Contents

On the title page: Stanley Clarkson as Don Basilio in *The Barber of Seville*. (Sadler's Wells Opera, 1960)

Introduction

Singing and acting have been part of the heritage of mankind from the dawn of history. Many different types of musical drama have been introduced, developed, transformed and transcended as new generations have added their creative contributions. Yet the underlying assumption has remained the same: that music makes theatrical performance more interesting and more powerful. Opera is one of the most exciting combinations of these vital elements of theatre.

The plays of the ancient Greeks are of special interest to us, for they were the models upon which the earliest operas were based. Music played some part in the lighter plays or comedies and a significant part in the serious plays or tragedies, although it is not known whether the plays were sung throughout. Certainly the choruses, which divided the plays into sections (corresponding to a modern act or scene), were sung. The melodies were accompanied by primitive string and wind instruments.

During the Middle Ages these ancient plays were forgotten. Travelling groups of players made a bare living by wandering from place to place and putting on theatrical performances in which music certainly played a part. However, since none of these plays was written down, we know very little about them.

We know more about the religious drama (liturgical drama) which arose during the 11th century. These plays originated in church as short sung dramatic presentations of the Easter story and of other Bible stories, and they used the hymns of the church service as the greater part of their material. In time the plays grew so long that they could no longer be performed during a church service. Then they were performed outdoors, often on the church steps, which functioned as a natural theatre. Another important change occurred at this time. As the plays grew longer, speaking was introduced between the musical numbers, and the plays, which were originally in Latin, began to be performed in the language of the people. Some songs were sung by soloists or the leading actors and others were sung by choruses.

A religious drama is performed in the streets before an eager crowd.

Organs probably were used to accompany the singing when the plays were performed in church. Later string and wind instruments were used.

While religious plays were developing in the church, other musical and dramatic activities were becoming popular at the courts of wealthy Italians. This was a by-product of the great flowering of the arts in Italy between 1400 and 1600 stimulated by interest and admiration for the artistic achievement of antiquity and known as the Renaissance. During the sixteenth century it became popular to produce classical plays, either in the original language or in Italian translation. Between the acts there were lavish spectacles involving singing, acting, dancing, instrumental music, costumes and sets. Unlike an opera, however, these presentations usually did not have a dramatic plot. Instead they elaborated an idea or theme. This kind of performance was called an *intermedio* or *intermezzo* because it came between the acts of the play.

Another popular entertainment was the *pastorale*. This was written in Italian but patterned after a classical poetic form which told stories of nymphs and shepherds and their interaction with gods and goddesses. Music was used for certain songs between sections of spoken dialogue. Bothe the *pastorale* and the *intermedio* certain elements that were incorporated into the earliest operas.

Towards the end of the sixteenth century a group of talented men met together at the home of Count Bardi in Florence. This group, called the 'Camerata', was interested in reviving in a modern style the powerful drama and music of the ancient Greeks, who had, they felt, achieved the ideal union of words and music. This led to the writing of the first opera, *Dafne*, in 1597 by the composer Jacopo Peri and the poet Ottavio Rinuccini. From the few fragments that survive, we know that *Dafne* had a theme like that of a *pastorale*, but unlike a *pastorale* it was sung throughout. Although the musical style was fairly uniform throughout the work, there was apparently some distinction made between the dialogue, which was set in a reciting style or *recitative*, and the songs, which were more melodic.

Although there were to be many changes in style and in content during the history of opera, the basic form had been achieved: a drama which is sung rather than spoken or declaimed, in which acting, music, dance, costumes, sets and special effects all play a part.

Today we have many opportunities to enjoy the fruits of almost 400 years of opera composition. Opera performances take place not only in major cities but in many smaller communities. Radio and television productions are frequent, and recordings are available of all major operas and of many obscure works as well. Never before has it been possible for so many to enjoy this major expression of Western culture.

Going to the Opera

Operas are written in many different languages. In some cases they are in musical styles that may sound strange to the uninitiated. In addition they rely heavily upon conventions: they do not portray life exactly as it is but instead use various musical and dramatic devices to convey their meaning. As a result, many young people—and their parents—approach opera with a kind of reverence bordering on fear. They wonder—and rightly—what is the best approach to take in preparing to go to the opera for the first time.

Familiarity with the plot and action of an opera is essential to enjoying the performance. Even those with many years of musical training and of foreign language study enjoy an opera more if they are thoroughly familiar with it. An ideal approach is to read a summary of the action of the opera and then to listen to the opera while following the libretto (text) with an English translation. More advanced musicians might prefer to follow the musical score of the opera. Opera recordings are available at most public libraries for loan, and most include a libretto and translation. It is important to realize that the more familiar you are with the music and the text, the more you will be able to enjoy the opera in performance.

Some operas, needless to say, are more immediately understandable than others. *Hänsel und Gretel* by Humperdinck, *Carmen* by Bizet, *Peter Grimes* or *The Turn of the Screw* by Britten, *Amahl and the Night Visitors* by Menotti, *Aïda* by Verdi, *La Bohème* by Puccini, *Il barbiere di Siviglia* by Rossini, or *Le nozze di Figaro* or *Don Giovanni* by Mozart are all good introductions to opera for young people.

Opera Production-
Backstage Today

An opera is not only a musical score and a play. Before an opera can be performed in front of an audience, dedicated artisans must devote many long hours of work to sets, lights, costumes, props and hundreds of other details. Arrangements must be made to schedule singers and directors. Repertory must be chosen. Without question the production of opera is the most complicated stage business of the twentieth century, and preparations for a single production often must begin more than three years before the first performance. One of the more complicated tasks of most opera houses is choosing the so-called 'repertory'. This is the collective name for the various operas chosen

Opposite: The audience awaits the start of a performance in the old Metropolitan Opera House. (New York, 1938)

Above: A view of Lincoln Center Plaza with the new Metropolitan Opera House in the centre.

for repeated performance over several seasons. Usually a chosen work will remain in the repertory for a period of years. Different casts will perform the work, but they will follow the precedent of earlier performances, and the technical aspects of the production – sets, costumes, lights etc. – will remain the same. Many larger resident companies, such as the Metropolitan Opera Company of New York City, follow this pattern. At the Met, twenty to twenty-four different operas are usually presented in a thirty-week season. Of these, perhaps four or five are new productions, while the rest are repeated from previous years. The other way for a company to organize its performance schedule is exemplified by the Festival Opera at Glyndebourne, England. A specific cast of performers is chosen for all performances of an opera during a season, and the work is not necessarily repeated in subsequent years. At Glyndebourne five different operas are usually presented during a ten-week season – usually two entirely new

11

productions and three rivivals of works done in previous years.

Both the Metropolitan Opera Company and the Glyndebourne Festival Opera send a touring company on the road to perform in other theatres in their own countries and also abroad, following the end of their regular season at home.

The Metropolitan Opera House of New York opened in 1883, under the patronage of a group of recently wealthy American millionaires who were unable to obtain boxes at the smaller Academy of Music, which had provided opera for the New York audience since 1849. None of the men who invested in the House expected it to be a paying financial venture, and none of them cared, because their main interest was in the social prestige it lent to their already secure financial positions. Fortunately the opera house gradually passed into the control of men whose major concerns were the artistic aspects of opera production, and the Met soon developed a reputation as one of the foremost centres of opera in the world. With its move in 1966 to a superbly designed facility in the new Lincoln Center for the Performing Arts in New York City, optimum conditions for the performance of opera on the grand scale were achieved.

The Festival Opera House at Glyndebourne, on the other hand, was the creation of one man. The imaginative and wealthy eccentric Captain John Christie decided to build an opera theatre at his country house in Sussex for the purpose of performing opera in ideal conditions. Christie himself became actively interested in music only when he was already over forty years old, when he began to organize regular performances of chamber music in the 'organ room' of his house during the late 1920s. An obvious admiration of Wagner and of the *Festspielhaus* at Bayreuth led him to branch out into opera production, and his wife, the soprano Audrey Mildmay, encouraged him to expand his project. The result was a fine theatre of acoustic excellence which incorporated the best of contemporary stagecraft in the design of its performance facilities. Christie was fortunate in his choice of Fritz Busch as music director and in Carl Ebert as producer. These two men shared a vision of the ideal opera performance, which included extensive rehearsals and extremely careful attention to all details of sets, costumes and lighting. When, after World War II, Christie's personal fortune could no longer support the theatre, several groups were organized to provide financial backing for the enterprise. Since that time rehearsal and storage facilities have been improved, the stage and lighting systems have been revamped, and the auditorium has been increased in size to permit the seating of a somewhat larger audience. At present the theatre seats 800 (a small audience compared to the gigantic capacity of the Met's 3,800 seats), contributing to the sense of intimacy that Christie so desired.

12

Opera-goers stroll on the lawns at Glyndebourne where the Festival Opera House blends elegantly with the private home of the Christie family.

Despite their disparate origins, the Met and Glyndebourne have many characteristics in common. Both are dedicated to excellence in operatic performance and both exploit their individual strengths to achieve this goal. Glyndebourne takes advantage of its intimate theatre and exceptional rehearsal possibilities to present completely integrated performances. Chamber operas and operas designed for smaller theatres, such as the Mozart operas, show to greatest advantage here. Because of the smaller financial gamble, Glyndebourne can afford to mount productions of more obscure or experimental works than the Met can. For example, the current popularity of Rossini's *La Cenerentola* (*Cinderella*) and *L'Italiana in Algeri* (*The Italian Girl in Algiers*) can be traced to their Glyndebourne revivals in the 1950s. The Met, on the other hand, takes advantage of its enormous stage and extremely sophisticated stage equipment to produce the theatrical effects required by such monumental works as Verdi's *Aïda*. Because of its leadership in opera production, it is able to offer the public the opportunity to hear the world's greatest singers of opera. The Met is also capable of producing during a season at

13

least four times as many operas as are produced at the Glyndebourne Festival, offering a much greater variety to the opera-going public.

Unified design for opera production was first developed by the composer Richard Wagner (1813–83). Designers are now employed to oversee all aspects of sets, lighting, costumes, makeup and all other essential areas of a production, so that an opera may be planned in its entirety. Previously, although singers certainly were chosen to complement each other, it was more common for standard sets to be used in a multitude of productions. Costumes were usually supplied by the singers. The concept of opera as an artistic whole did not exist.

With most opera companies today, a production is designed as a unit. At the Metropolitan Opera and at Glyndebourne, repertory for a season is usually chosen at least three years in advance and singers are offered contracts. A designer or group of designers begins work, and their plans are turned over to the various opera shops to be translated into reality as costumes, wigs or props. Every detail must be considered. How long will it take to change the sets between scenes? How is each special effect, such as smoke or snow, to be achieved?

The Metropolitan Opera is somewhat unusual in that all its production work is done in its own shops. In other words, it does not contract such things as sets or costumes to outside agencies but instead employs a large group of people on a regular basis throughout the year to produce these things. At Glyndebourne as well, virtually all the costumes, wigs and props are made in Glyndebourne's own shops. An exception might be that if a production required a large number of military uniforms, for example, these would be ordered from a specialist military tailor in London. Likewise the sets, which are built in Sussex, are sent up to London to large studios to be painted. They are then returned to Glyndebourne, where the finishing touches are added. Heads of departments, such as wardrobe, work year round, while others work on a seasonal basis as needed.

A glimpse into the various shops at the Met will give an idea of how the 'magic' of a staged opera is achieved. The shops are all located in the opera house itself, close to the backstage areas.

In the scenic shop, drawings for the sets are enlarged and painted on enormous sheets of canvas stretched on frames. These are sometimes underlaid with thin plywood to make them sturdier. In this two-storey room there is a fascinating motorized stretcher frame, which is used in painting the gigantic backdrops of the stage. The canvas backdrop is attached to a frame which can be raised or lowered by pulleys, making it possible to paint all of the immense area without using scaffolding. This shop is also in charge of such special effects as making costumes look old

A backdrop for *La Gioconda* being painted by members of the
Met's scenic department. The canvas is attached to an 'elevator'
frame which allows it to be raised or lowered for ease of painting.

(this is more difficult than it sounds!) by brushing them with wire
brushes, or cutting them, or carefully staining them.

In the adjoining carpentry shop, staircases and rocks are constructed in
detachable and folding sections so that they can be loaded into the freight
elevator and efficiently moved from storage to stage or can be loaded
into trucks and moved to the warehouse or taken along on the

company's spring tour. An interesting detail is that steps are padded for silence, then covered with canvas and returned to the scenic shop, where they are painted to resemble wood or stone.

In the electrical shop all the lighting fixtures for the stage are made, from elaborate chandeliers for party scenes in elegant ballrooms to small electrical candles carried by the chorus in processions. This shop also does all of the wiring required for special effects – the fan system for blowing 'smoke' (achieved with dry ice) across the stage, for example.

The prop shop turns out the most fascinating items of all: the trick sword that falls apart when struck, the witch's oven that explodes in *Hänsel und Gretel*. Here they make large yet lightweight trees and classical stone columns of foam sprayed with a hardener. Small items are made of fiberglas – unbreakable goblets and jugs, for instance. Stage furniture and even curtains are made here, as are such trifles as a fan or a silver rose.

The costume shop makes all the costumes for the productions and also organizes and distributes them as they are needed for performances. Everything is custom-made in this shop, on the grounds that clothes that

---

Members of the Metropolitan Opera's tailor shop discussing a costume for *Anthony and Cleopatra*, designed by Franco Zeffirelli.

fit well last longer as well as look better. All the measurements of every performer, down to the last member of the chorus, are on file here. If the cast changes for a certain production, duplicate costumes or alterations can be made in advance. The inventiveness that is apparent in all the opera shops is demonstrated here by costumes which are designed to be transformed from act to act. A first-act gentleman can be transformed into a third-act general by the addition of a harness of braid and medals. Costumes of many periods require careful construction in order to appear appropriately substantial on stage, and sometimes this can only be achieved by the use of heavy fabrics. Often rare or unusual fabrics or embroidery must be found. Therefore it is a major task simply to obtain materials and to keep a record of inventory. In addition to creating costumes from the designer's plans, this department is in charge of keeping costumes in good repair and cleaning those stained by use and by the inevitable stage makeup. The wardrobe mistress and her staff make sure that costumes are available to performers for each dress rehearsal and performance, an undertaking that could easily utilize a computer.

Judith Blegen, soprano, being made up for the role of Sophie in a Met production of Strauss's *Der Rosenkavalier*.

The wig and makeup departments also work in conjunction with the designers of a production. The wig department must arrange to buy hair of appropriate colours and execute hair styles in a multitude of periods. Many wigs are now made of synthetic materials, but much human hair is still used because it is easier to restyle and to clean. The makeup department, while translating the designers' wishes into reality, must take into consideration such practical concerns as making sure that a singer can still breathe with his large putty nose, or that Madame Butterfly can still see when her eyes are given an oriental slant upwards by invisible tape. In most cases, the chorus members learn to apply their own makeup following the directions of the makeup staff.

The crew that manages the moving of sets to and from storage is composed of well-trained experts. Moving is extremely hard on scenery, and performances are scheduled so that it is moved as little as possible. While the Metropolitan Opera has storage space for approximately eight to twelve productions in the house itself, there may be as many as twenty or even twenty-four productions in a season. This means that some sets must be trucked in from outside warehouses when they are needed. An enormous freight elevator moves sets from this storage area up to stage level. The work of the crew is made easier by sets which are designed to be broken into several pieces for moving.

Lighting plays an important role in any production. At the Metropolitan Opera, in addition to the lights concealed behind the proscenium (the stage frame) and to special backstage lighting effects, there are three large light groups concealed in the ceiling of the auditorium. A control booth and viewing room for the lighting engineer is located at the back of the ground floor of the auditorium. Much of the lighting is controlled electronically, but cues must be arranged and lighting chosen to fit the overall design of the production. The lighting crew is responsible for such special effects as the dawning of a new day or the fading of the sun at evening.

The stage at the Metropolitan is actually four separate stages in one. The main stage (103' by 90') is divided into seven sections on independent elevator systems. The individual sections can be raised or lowered for special stage effects, or can be terraced to produce a stage slanted upwards towards the back. It is even possible to prepare a set below the main stage and lift it thirty feet from the basement to stage level. In addition, there are fifty-two trap doors to make it possible for artists to enter from or exit to the area under the stage. Small lifts carry the performers up and down.

Adjoining the main stage are two side stages and a stage directly behind the main stage. Each of these additional stages is on a wagon, so that it can be wheeled electrically into position on the main stage. This makes it possible to change scenes without any construction, and offers the added advantage that when two or more scenes spaced throughout an opera are set in the same location, the original set can simply be rolled again onto the main stage. Sound-proof curtains can be lowered between these stages, making it possible for a full dress rehearsal to take place on the main stage at the same time that a piano rehearsal of another opera is being held on one of the side stages. The back stage can be used in conjunction with the main stage to achieve greater depth and also features a revolving platform fifty-eight feet in diameter which can be used for special effects. The designers of a production consult with the technicians to decide which of the facilities of the opera house will be used.

As the physical preparations for a production approach completion and the date of the first performance draws near, rehearsals must begin. At the Met, the 78-member chorus may have begun to learn the music up to a year in advance, and the choreographers (designers or composers of dances) have made plans and begun work with the 24-member ballet corps. Soloists usually learn their roles independently. However, if it is a new role, a soloist may come to New York up to three weeks before the

A view of the Met's main stage looking out towards the auditorium.

performance to work with the opera company's coaches or 'répétiteurs' (people who help a singer with the musical and dramatic interpretation of a role). Before he works with a singer, a coach goes through the opera with the musical director, discussing problems of musical interpretation and cuts in the score, if there are to be any. The musical director and the stage director confer, and the stage director plans the blocking or action that will occur in the performance. Then the stage director begins work with the performers in a large rehearsal studio (the size of the main stage) where lines are taped or drawn to indicate positions of the sets.

Depending on the opera to be performed, there may be from two to fourteen days of piano rehearsals on the main stage and at least two orchestral rehearsals. Singers must have the opportunity to accustom themselves to the numerous performance details of a particular production, and technical cues (i.e., various signals to initiate lighting or scene changes) have to be established so that there will be few if any mix-ups in performance. Occasionally technical rehearsals are run for the sole purpose of arranging lighting and staging cues. Details such as quick changes of a performer's costume must be considered, and portable dressing rooms may be moved to the stage area if they are needed.

Stagehands play a vital part in any opera performance, working quietly and quickly to make scene changes the instant the curtain falls. Without their expertise it would be impossible to achieve the transformations of scene required in most operas.

Closed circuit TV is used to transmit cues from the musical director, who stands in the lowered orchestra pit in front of the stage, to the prompter, who sits in a hooded box at the centre front of the stage platform. The prompter performs an essential role in any opera production. He is responsible for cueing the singers on stage and for giving them their initial pitches so that they begin singing in the correct key. On occasion he may sing the beginning of every phrase of an entire role. This is particularly helpful to a singer who is doing a role in an unaccustomed language. Clearly the prompter must know the opera inside and out. If the singers do not feel they can depend on him, he is useless.

Closed circuit TV is also used to transmit cues from the musical director to an offstage chorus director on those numerous occasions in opera when a chorus either begins to sing offstage or sings an entire piece offstage. The chorus director must slightly anticipate the director's beat so that the sound from backstage, which has a longer distance to travel than the sound from the orchestra pit, will be synchronized with the rest of the musical score. Amplification is used during a performance mainly for special sound effects or for projecting a backstage chorus. Solo singers have been trained to project their voices to the very back of the large auditorium and do so without amplification.

In addition to the chorus, many operas use a number of extras or 'supers' (short for 'supernumeraries', as they are called in opera). These people, who help to fill the stage in crowd scenes, are often opera fans who 'super' regularly as a hobby. They don costumes and, usually without special rehearsal, imitate whatever the singing chorus does on stage (except sing, of course). Children, often relatives of people working in some capacity on a production, are occasionally included in this group, and children may also sing in the opera's children's chorus. Some operas even require children soloists, such as the three boys in Mozart's *Die Zauberflöte* (*The Magic Flute*).

To keep all of the backstage technical details under control, a group of stage managers is required. These people deal with such problems as when to raise and lower the curtain, give lighting and scene change cues, and call performers to the stage. In addition there are three to four *maestri*, depending on the work performed, who arrange to get the performers on to the stage itself on cue. Another person is solely in charge of the 'supers'.

The backstage areas are arranged as close to the stage as possible and are connected to the stage area by telephone and by a paging system. The dressing rooms for the soloists are very comfortable and almost homey. Each contains a washbasin and lighted makeup mirror, a piano and a *chaise longue*. Shower and restroom facilities adjoin each dressing room. There are special dressing areas for men and women chorus members and for the *corps de ballet*. Here performers keep their own makeup kits and regularly used shoes. Adjacent lounges provide them with an area in which to rest during long performances or rehearsals.

In most respects, production of an opera at Glyndebourne is similar to that at the Met. Glyndebourne, for example, was one of the first opera houses to utilize a closed circuit TV system. Particularly noteworthy is Glyndebourne's long and extensive rehearsal preparation. Contracts specify exactly when the singers are expected to arrive for rehearsals, and they are expected to arrive knowing their music thoroughly. The 1979 production of Beethoven's *Fidelio* offers an example of how much preparation goes into a single production. The chorus, which plays a considerable role in the opera, began work five weeks before opening night. The leads arrived to begin rehearsal only one week later. Lead singers were scheduled for two rehearsal sessions each day, six days a week. They began with musical rehearsals to work out ensembles and scenes. After four or five days of this, they began production rehearsals (staging rehearsals) accompanied by piano. Then the musical director for the production arrived, and more musical rehearsals were held to work out specific details. At the same time, evening rehearsals were being held to arrange lighting and other technical aspects of the production, a full ten

days before the performance dress rehearsals began. With such careful preparation, it is no wonder that some of the world's best operatic performances occur here.

Because of the great number of rehearsals, the removable prompter's box at Glyndebourne is rarely used. If an understudy (replacement) is taking over for a lead, a prompter and a member of the musical staff are posted at the side of the stage in case of problems. But since the understudies as well as the leads are well-prepared, problems seldom arise.

The chorus of the Glyndebourne Festival Opera is not a permanent professional group as it is at the Metropolitan. It is instead designed as a training ground for young English singers. A member of the Glyndebourne staff constantly searches out and auditions talented young singers from the colleges and conservatories of Great Britain and may hear up to three or four hundred singers a year for this purpose. Of these a certain number are chosen to come into the chorus, which has a turnover of roughly a third of the singers each year. After singing with the chorus for a year, a promising young singer may well be given an understudy role at the festival the following year or a small principal role with the touring company which goes on the road after the regular festival ends. The third year a talented singer may have a small principal role in the festival – such as Barbarina in *Le nozze di Figaro* (*The Marriage of Figaro*) – and a major role on the tour – perhaps Susanna in the same opera. Many well-known British singers, among them Peter Pears and Janet Baker, have sung in the Glyndebourne chorus.

Despite their somewhat differing approaches and their different facilities and goals, one common characteristic stands out in both the Glyndebourne Festival Opera and the Metropolitan Opera: an intense feeling of family unity. Everyone who works with these opera companies has an almost tangible love of opera, which is apparent in their enthusiasm and dedication to their jobs. The hours are long indeed, and the pay is not always entirely compensatory for the time away from family and friends. An opera therefore does not just consist of singers and performers. It is a large group of dedicated people who pull together to stage one of our most complicated and elaborate art forms.

Opposite above: A Glyndebourne Festival Opera production rehearsal for *Fidelio*. Producer Sir Peter Hall (centre) and conductor Bernard Haitink (foreground, left), with singers Curt Appelgren ('Rocco') and Elisabeth Söderström ('Leonore').

Opposite below: The Epilogue to Stravinsky's *The Rake's Progress* performed at Glyndebourne in 1978 with sets by David Hockney.

An Opera Singer Today -
Nicolai Gedda

Born in Sweden of a Swedish mother and a Russian father, Nicolai Gedda is one of the leading operatic tenors of today. Having sung as a chorister when he was a boy, he first listened to great Italian tenors such as Gigli and Schipa on the radio when he was a student. They made an enormous impact on him, and it was not long before he found a teacher in Sweden and set out on the path to becoming an opera singer. He studied with the aid of a grant after winning the highest prize in the Christine Nilsson awards for young singers and made his professional début in 1952. Here he talks about his career as an opera singer and the sort of life style it involves.

Becoming an Opera Singer

Three things are absolutely essential: the first (and most important) is that you have a good voice by nature; the second is that you find a good teacher; and the third is that your health and nerves are good. After that it is sheer luck. I found a good teacher, and I had the opportunity to learn stagecraft and musicianship with good teachers. It takes time to become a singer, and I would advise young singers not to be in a hurry, because you can't learn singing and you can't achieve a solid technique in two or three weeks. It takes years. I was actually taking singing lessons for fifteen years after my début. A voice has to be polished all the time, like a diamond. Because we are only human, we singers easily fall into bad habits and need a good teacher who can hear us – another ear, so to speak – to stop us wandering from the right path. Now that my own teachers have died, I am on my own, but by now I feel that my vocal technique is so solid that I can work by myself. All the recordings that I make are a great help, because this way I have the opportunity really to hear myself. I work at the piano with my vocalizing, and I think a lot too: am I doing this right? Am I doing this specific exercise right? Am I doing something wrong? Or does it feel right? And so on. It requires constant polishing, constant working.

24

Nicolai Gedda as Lensky in *Eugene Onegin*, one of his favourite operatic roles.

Of course, a singer must also know languages, because nowadays theatres are doing their operas in original languages – so Italian, French and German are essential. He or she should be able not only to pronounce them, but also to understand them.

The Life Style of a Singer

Sleep is extremely important, and I myself need at least eight hours of sleep a night to feel all right. Exercise is also very important, as singers work at night and usually eat after their performances and have weight problems as a result. I usually exercise for fifteen or twenty minutes every morning. Jogging is also good, but it must be in good weather, or one could easily get a cold. Singers do everything they can to avoid colds, but it is very difficult not to catch them, especially with the air pollution we have today.

On an 'average day' when I do not have a performance, I usually sit down at the piano and do some vocalizing for twenty minutes or half an

Relaxing at home, 1976.

hour, especially if I have to do some coaching that day. To learn something new, I always want to warm up a little; but sometimes I feel so good that I don't have to warm up. I also believe in having a few days of rest, just to leave my instrument, my voice, in peace and quiet.

The Day of the Performance

On the day of a performance, I take it easy. If it's a difficult opera, I want to keep quiet as much as possible and not talk too much. I have a late breakfast – a brunch – with eggs and a little ham and coffee, so that it's a good meal. Then I don't eat any lunch and I don't eat any dinner. (After the performance I'm not very hungry either, so I keep my weight down this way.) After brunch, I rest a little, and then do about half an hour of vocalizing. That will be about 1:00 in the afternoon. For the rest of the afternoon I rest and concentrate on my assignment for the evening. I go through in my mind a few things I have to remember; I may look through the score; or I may just lie down and think about it and concentrate. Around 6:00, I vocalize again, and then go to the theatre at least an hour before the performance to be made up, to be dressed, and again, to concentrate on the role I will sing that evening.

Recording an opera presents special problems for a singer, because the technical equipment today is so sensitive that any little blemish on the voice is heard. You have to come to the recording session in top shape, and so I personally prepare for every recording by working on my voice and getting it in shape by vocalizing even more thoroughly than usual.

Rehearsing with Gerald Moore, 1973.

Learning a New Role

I begin by learning the music and the text. While you are doing that you already have an idea of what is going on on stage in the different scenes, duets and ensembles. But I think the most important thing for the singer is to be as secure as possible musically before beginning the stage rehearsals.

Because of lack of time and money, people in responsible positions in theatres, the conductors and directors, just aren't able to work on simple things. The singers have to be prepared, because there is not enough time even for necessary rehearsals. So I spend a lot of time on learning the music and also thinking of different dramatic expressions I can use – different 'colours' of the voice. After I have learned the score I can begin stage rehearsals. You get together with the stage director, who tells you about his conception of the whole opera. Usually the conductor is present, and together you can discuss the musical problems. But even when you get to the dress rehearsals, there are still problems to be solved – acoustical problems or problems of contact with the conductor. Singers don't like a perfect or a very good dress rehearsal. We feel that during a dress rehearsal all kinds of, well, not precisely disasters, but all kinds of things should happen. We prefer to have a lapse of memory or a vocal problem happen during the dress rehearsal, because then we can concentrate on that problem and avoid it during the performance. There is always the danger that if a dress rehearsal is perfect, we relax too much for the performance. Not all performances are successful – where public and singers are both happy – and great performances are rare. The most exciting and rewarding part of my profession is when the conception of the stage director and the performance by the singers harmonizes, and on opening night you feel that you have the public with you – that you have not only the sympathy, but the enthusiasm of the public. You feel that you have made an impact on them. This is certainly the most exciting aspect of my work, because you can never predict the public's reaction. Suddenly the whole atmosphere can change. The reactions of the public – its laughter, its applause after a successful scene, the lack of reaction where you expected it, or a reaction you didn't expect – this is the most exciting aspect of being a singer.

Favourite Roles

I don't really have any favourite operatic role. But I enjoy singing Lensky in *Eugene Onegin*. Tchaikovsky is a favourite composer of mine, and the role is very beautiful to sing. It's a role that has, I would guess, many of the ingredients of my own character. Lensky is a poet with a good deal of temperament. He has a wonderful quarrel scene with Onegin during the Larins' ball. He shows a typical Russian melancholy in the duel scene. More and more this opera is done in the original Russian. I have done it in English, but the new performances in Russian at the Met and at Covent Garden are much more successful.

Favourite Opera Houses

I like to sing with the Metropolitan Opera in New York and with Covent Garden in London, and also at the Royal Opera in my home town, Stockholm, and in many of the Italian theatres. I especially enjoy working at the Met because the preparation is so good there. This is not the case in other theatres I could mention. In some you get maybe one rehearsal, and not even all the singers come. Today I refuse to do those things any more – I don't have the nerves for it, and I don't think it is fair to the public for me to sing in an unfamiliar production and just walk around and guess things on stage. I did it very often when I was younger; and I was fairly successful at it, and I even enjoyed the challenge. But there is no question that the performance suffers, and it is not fair to the public. Certainly it makes the achievement of an exciting, ideal performance difficult if not impossible.

The Operas

The Early Aristocratic Tradition of Opera – Monteverdi

Among the earliest operas still performed today is *La favola d'Orfeo* (*The Myth of Orpheus*) by Claudio Monteverdi (1567–1643), who wrote it while serving as court musician to the Duke of Mantua. It was first performed in Mantua, Italy, on February 22, 1607. The libretto (text), written by Alessandro Striggio, tells the story of the minstrel Orfeo and his lovely wife Euridice. The story is taken from a Greek myth that was well known by the educated people of the time, and in keeping with the tradition of contemporary literature, characters include not only gods and goddesses and other figures from mythology, but also personifications of such abstract qualities as Love and Hope.

The opera begins with a short instrumental piece, which introduces the play in much the same way that longer overtures do in later works. Next comes a prologue, or sung introduction to the play, by Music himself, who tells us that the opera to follow is about Orpheus, assuming that we are all familiar with this story.

In Act 1. Orfeo sings of his great happiness with Euridice, his beautiful wife (*Rosa del ciel, vita del mondo – Rose of the sky, life of the world*) to a group of assembled nymphs and shepherds. The act ends with singing and dancing by all.

Act 2. is introduced by a short sinfonia, or instrumental interlude, a feature which occurs throughout this opera. Euridice has left, but Orfeo still sings of his happiness to the nymphs and shepherds (*Vi ricorda, o boschi ombrosa – Do you remember, O shadowy woods?*). Suddenly a nymph enters with the tragic news that Euridice has been fatally bitten by a serpent (*Ahi, caso acerbo – Alas, bitter grief*). Orfeo laments her and decides to follow her to Hades, the kingdom of the dead, in a song ending with the words 'Addio terra, addio cielo, e sole, addio' (*Farewell earth, farewell sky, and sun, farewell*). The nymphs and shepherds mourn with him, echoing the words of the nymph who brought the sad news (*Ahi, caso acerbo*).

In Act 3. Orfeo enters with Hope, who is guiding him to Hades. As they reach the gate of this dread kingdom, Orfeo is left alone to confront Charon, the boatman who ferries the souls of the dead across the River Styx to the underworld. Charon is reluctant to take a living man across, but Orfeo sings so beautifully (*Possente spirto – Powerful spirit*) that Charon falls asleep. Orfeo crosses into Hades where the spirits are amazed at his audacity.

In Act 4. Proserpina, the Queen of Hades, begs Pluto, the King, to permit the couple to return to the land of the living. Pluto yields to her pleading, but only on the condition that Orfeo will not turn back to look at Euridice as she follows him out of Hades. If he once looks back, she

A scene from the 1970 Sadler's Wells Opera production of Monteverdi's *Orfeo* with Alexander Young in the title role and John Winfield as Apollo.

A caricature of Francesco Senesino (a famous *castrato*), with
Francesca Cuzzoni and Gaetan Berenstat in Haňdel's *Flavio*. (King's
Theatre, 1723)

will be lost to him forever. Orfeo, knowing of this condition, nevertheless turns back to see if Euridice is actually following him, and at once
darkness falls on them both. The spirits of the dead tell him that he will
never see Euridice again.

In Act 5. Orfeo has returned alone to earth in sorrow (*Questi i campi di
Tracia – Here are the fields of Thrace*), and only a lonely echo answers his
song. But Apollo, the god of light, has not forgotten him and appears to
take him to heaven as a consolation. The shepherds rejoice with singing
and dancing at his renewed happiness.

Venice – The First Public Opera House

During the first half of the 17th century many operas were composed and performed in the courts of Italy, but none of these remain in the regular opera repertory of today. It was the opening of the first public opera house, the Teatro di San Cassiano in Venice, which established opera as a popular form of entertainment. As a result of this public theatre, Venetian opera became the central force in opera in the 17th century, under the leadership of such composers as Monteverdi, Cavalli and Marc Antonio Cesti. History and mythology – the standard sources of plots – were modified in order to heighten their dramatic interest. Mistaken identity and chance encounters became stock features. Stagecraft specialized in marvellous machines for stage effects, which included the descents and ascents of the omnipresent gods and goddesses. A dramatic power replaced the gentler and more pastoral quality of the earlier operas. For example, Monteverdi's *L'incoronazione di Poppea* (*The Coronation of Poppea* – 1642), which was first performed in the Teatro di San Cassiano, uses subtle harmonic means as well as a dramatic melodic style to interpret the grisly story in which the Roman emperor Nero banishes his best general and divorces his wife in order to make his mistress, Poppea, empress.

During the last half of the 17th century, opera tended to develop a specific set of musical forms. The short instrumental piece or sinfonia which introduced *La favola d'Orfeo* developed into a full scale overture, which contained themes from, or indicated the character of, the work to follow. It was composed in two parts: a slow introduction followed by a faster section. The *da capo* aria was also a two-part form: a beginning section, followed by a second section with different music and text, followed in turn by a repetition of the first section, possibly in abridged or ornamented form.

Contemporary accounts of this period of opera emphasize the number of scene changes and the elaborate stage machinery. Clearly the audience demanded – and got – spectacle. The parts were sung by men, women and *castrati* (male sopranos or altos). A *castrato* voice was the result of castrating a promising boy singer before he reached puberty. This produced a man's voice in colour and power, with the range of a boy's – quite a different effect from the clear and lyric sound of a countertenor voice, which is a man's trained falsetto. In their heyday, famous *castrati* were the pampered darlings of the opera-going public, and they continued to be popular well into the 19th century, although Rossini (1792–1868) was the last major operatic composer to write music for them. Today a *castrato* role is usually sung by a female contralto.

Early Opera in France and England – Lully and Purcell

Opera, an Italian invention, spread to other countries of Europe and was adapted and interpreted according to the traditions and demands of individual nations. France already had at that time a highly developed tradition in several art forms: (1) the French classical tragedy (typified by the plays of Corneille and Racine); (2) the pastorale; and (3) the ballet (which grew out of the dance of the French court). Jean-Baptiste Lully (1632–1687) was clever enough to combine these three elements into an intrinsically French form of opera. Taking over the Académie Royale de Musique in Paris in 1673, he presented a long series of operas from then until his death in 1687. His libretti were faithful to the text of the tragedies he chose to set, and every effort was made to present the words in a clear and comprehensible manner. The operas are largely composed of recitative, that is, recitation of the text to a very simple melody, occasionally moving into simple airs which are quite unlike the more developed Italian arias. The chorus and the ballet played a significant role, and the overture developed its characteristic 'French overture' form: a slow beginning section in dotted rhythm, followed by a faster section often in fugal form, in which one part imitates another. Lully had an immense effect on the development of French opera, which for the next century followed the pattern he set.

A court masque (1550). Elaborately costumed mythological characters are accompanied by flutes, viols, lutes and drums.

England at that time also had what amounted to a national form of entertainment: the court masque. This was allegorical in subject matter and owed much to the ballet in its origin. The major emphasis was on costumes and spectacle. Spoken dialogue was interspersed with songs and dances, and consequently early English attempts at opera most often took the form of plays with music.

One of England's greatest composers, Henry Purcell (1659–1695), made a unique experiment in the composition of a chamber opera, *Dido and Aeneas*. The opera is based on the section of Virgil's *Aeneid* in which Dido, Queen of Carthage, and Aeneas, who is destined to found the city of Rome, meet, fall in love and are parted by the machinations of the gods. Its libretto is by Nahum Tate.

The work, first performed in 1689, was written for a girls' school rather than for a public stage, and perhaps for this reason Purcell felt free to ignore many of the standard musical and dramatic conventions of the time. The chorus plays an important role, commenting on the action of the play, giving emphasis to the words of the soloists, and dominating the end of scenes and acts. As in the masque, many dances are included. The opera is composed largely in recitative style, which becomes more melodic in dramatic or emotional situations. The dialogue reveals a remarkable amount of interaction between characters, particularly when Aeneas is on stage. In addition to several duets there are a number of full-scale arias, some of which – at moments of particularly intense foreboding – are constructed on a ground bass (a repeating bass line over which the singer's melody is woven). A *continuo* (an uninterrupted bass line which dominates the overall construction of the music) is heard throughout, giving the opera remarkable cohesiveness and dramatic intensity.

The overture begins in a stately and foreboding manner which suggests the tragic character of this work. A second faster section follows (but the parts do not imitate each other as in the 'French overture' of Lully).

Act 1. begins in Dido's palace in Carthage. Belinda, Dido's sister, sings '*Shake the cloud from off your brow*', in an attempt to cheer Dido. The queen answers in turn, in an air on a ground bass (*Ah! Belinda*), that she suffers a secret anguish. Belinda tells her that she is aware of Dido's love for Aeneas, and in a charming duet with an attendant she encourages the match (*Fear no danger*). Aeneas enters to tell Dido of his love for her. At first reluctant, Dido is eventually won over by Aeneas, with Belinda's assistance (*Pursue thy conquest love*). The scene ends with a triumphant chorus (*To the hills and the vales*) followed by a dance.

Scene 2. takes place in a cave. A scary, slow prelude with a falling melodic pattern sets the stage for the entrance of the sorceress. She calls forth the witches, who arrive with a truly wicked sounding chorus (*Harm's our delight*). She explains that she has arranged that Jove, the king of the gods, will send Aeneas word that he must depart at once with his fleet; meanwhile they are to conjure up a storm to spoil the hunting in which the lovers are now engaged. In a concluding chorus (*In our deep vaulted cell*), the witches retire to their cave to practice their wicked spells.

Act 2. takes place in a pastoral grove, and the mood is indicated by a lyrical prelude. Belinda describes the lovely scene, echoed by the chorus (*Thanks to these lonesome vales*). A note of foreboding is struck by the tense and nervous aria (on a ground bass) sung by a woman of the court. As the storm descends, Belinda and the chorus urge the lovers, just returned from the hunt, to seek shelter in town. The spirit of the sorceress in the guise of Mercury comes to Aeneas and announces that Jove has ordered him to leave at once. Reluctantly, Aeneas agrees to do so.

As Act 3. begins, Aeneas and his sailors are preparing to embark. The sorceress and the witches arrive, gloating over their success and making plans for storms to drown Aeneas once he is at sea. Dido and Belinda

Sandra Browne and Christian du Plessis in the title roles of Purcell's *Dido and Aeneas*. (English National Opera, 1979)

enter with Aeneas. He is now wavering in his resolve to leave, but Dido tells him that since he once considered abandoning her, he must now go. As Aeneas departs, the chorus sings '*Great minds against themselves conspire*', and Dido prepares herself for death in a moving aria (*When I am laid in earth*) sung over a descending chromatic ground bass, in which the bass line slowly moves by half steps down the scale. The chorus concludes the opera (*With drooping wings*), taking up the falling line of Dido's melody and eventually breaking into melodic 'sighs' which die away at the end.

Baroque Opera in England – Händel

In 1710 the young composer Georg Frideric Händel (1685–1759) arrived in England from Germany, where he had already won a reputation as a composer of *opera seria* (serious or tragic opera). Over a period of thirty

The Drottningholm Court Theatre in Sweden, an original Baroque theatre shown here with stage settings by Carlo Bibiena, made about 1760. Note the exceptionally deep stage and elaborate perspective.

years he wrote forty operas for his English audience, all to Italian texts, and thus he found himself in the curious position of being a German who represented Italian culture to the English public. Despite the rage for Italian singers in this period, opera was never firmly established in England, and Händel's operas brought him fame but little fortune.

Händel retained most of the traditional forms that had arisen in earlier operas, especially those of Lully and the Italian composer Alessandro Scarlatti (1660–1725). These included the 'French overture' (which was occasionally followed by one or more additional movements), *secco* recitative ('dry' recitative, accompanied by a few chords on the harpsichord) and the *da capo* aria. This aria form, though static from the dramatic point of view, provided an ideal vehicle for the extremely admired and much applauded Italian singers of Händel's day, since it gave them an opportunity to show off their ability to improvise a second set of musical ornaments during the repetition of the first section. In many respects Händel was a genius at showing off a singer's voice, which

Janet Baker in the title role of Händel's *Julius Caesar* (English National Opera, 1979). An English mezzo-soprano, she first appeared in opera at Oxford in 1956 and has since acquired an international reputation as a concert and opera singer.

was exactly what the public wanted. His use of instruments to contrast with the colour of the human voice is one of his trademarks. His choruses are monumental in scale and often contrapuntal in design (that is, each voice part carries an independent melody). Sections of instrumental music are included for dances or processions.

Opera seria did not intend to present a realistic picture of events or of characters and their interaction. Rather, it tried to portray pure, unmixed and unadulterated emotions. A character will display first Anger, then Despair, then Resolution, but transitions between these states are not explored. Specific musical devices and aria styles were devised to present these emotions in a consistent and uniform manner from opera to opera. A leaping bass line, for example, is the standard accompaniment for an aria of Vengeance. Händel further developed this dramatic system by the introduction of the *grand scena*. This was a dramatic unit composed of a variety of musical elements: *secco* recitative and *accompagnato* recitative (recitative accompanied by the orchestra); *arioso* sections, which were more melodic than recitative but did not achieve the proportions of a

The Beggar's Opera in London, 1728 (as depicted by Hogarth): Lavinia Fenton, an English soprano and actress, was the first Polly Peachum (kneeling).

full-scale aria; and, of course, an elaborate *da capo* aria. These elements were strung together according to the dramatic needs of the scene and formed a dramatic whole rather than an unconnected sequence of events.

Many of Händel's operas, including the strongly dramatic *Giulio Cesare* (1724), have been revived to the delight of 20th-century audiences. Others are *Rinaldo* (1711), *Rodelinda* (1725), and *Alcina* (1735). Many aspects of Händel's operas, because of their grandiose and pretentious nature, lent themselves to parody, and writers of the time were not slow to point out their defects. In 1728 a musical satire was introduced at the Lincoln's Inn Fields Theatre. *The Beggar's Opera* by John Gay and John Christopher Pepusch made an instant hit with the London public, who were marvellously entertained by the choice of characters in the work. Instead of a king or a hero, a highwayman played the leading part, supported by other characters from the lowest levels of society. The overture draws melodies from the work itself and sets a light tone. In essence *The Beggar's Opera* is not really an opera at all, but rather a play with music drawn from many sources. Among them are popular songs and even a melody from Händel's opera *Rinaldo*. The sentiments expressed in the work are remarkably pretentious for such a ragamuffin set of characters, and the work is thoroughly delightful in its simple way. It did show that the English play with music was a viable art form and left a legacy to English stage music in the 19th-century works of Gilbert and Sullivan.

Opera Reform in the 18th Century – Gluck

Christoph Willibald von Gluck (1714–1787) is credited with a major reform of serious opera. Born in Bavaria, he spent his early years in Prague and Vienna, where he met many composers of *opera seria* and heard their works. From 1750 to 1762 he travelled widely on the Continent and in England, composing operas that were not very different from those of his contemporaries. He became familiar with the French *opéra comique*, which was a play with music. In an earlier period its music had consisted of popular songs fitted out with new texts, but by Gluck's time both play and music were written as a unit. Gluck himself wrote music for this unpretentious type of opera, learning by experience the difficult art of setting French in a syllabic style to a simple and restrained melody.

At the same time that Gluck was writing music for the *opéra comique*, new ideas about art were circulating, including the notion that music should form a vehicle for simple and free expression of feelings. The baroque opera of Händel had deliberately constructed emotional fictions: its characters were limited to portraying pure emotions in which only one aspect of an emotional state could be revealed at a time. Now naturalness was in vogue; audiences wanted to see human beings portrayed in all their emotional complexity. Gluck believed that he could translate this into musical terms.

The emphasis on forms and formality of the previous age were among the elements subjected to change. The elaborate metaphors of the Baroque texts give way to a clearer, more restrained language. The elegant vocal passages of runs, trills and other vocal ornaments (coloratura) so beloved of Baroque singers are simplified to make clear musical speech possible. The *da capo* aria is replaced with shorter airs which grow naturally out of the dramatic situation; word repetition occurs only for emphasis, although the last line of an aria is occasionally repeated to form a final cadence. Sections of *accompagnato* recitative (*secco* recitative was banished from the style) alternate with sections of aria. The two forms are still distinct in that the recitative is more dramatic and compelling, while the aria is more lyrical and melodic. Overall, however, there is less contrast between the individual sections, and a strong sense of musical unity. The orchestra is no longer used to contrast with the voice but instead to support it. Only the ballet continues relatively unchanged.

The librettist Ranieri da Calzabigi (1714–1795) worked closely with Gluck to produce *Orfeo ed Euridice* (*Orpheus and Euridice*), the first masterpiece in this style, which was premièred at the Burgtheater in Vienna on October 5, 1762. The story is based on the old Greek myth of Orpheus which Monteverdi had chosen to set nearly 150 years earlier (see pp. 30–32), but Gluck's treatment of it is novel in many respects.

After an overture reflecting the serious character of the work to follow, Act 1. begins in front of the tomb of Euridice, Orfeo's dead wife. As Orfeo sings of his sorrow, Love enters to tell him that Jove, king of the gods, has taken pity on him; he will permit Orfeo to descend to Hades with his lyre to reclaim Euridice, but on one condition: if he turns back to look at her, she will be lost to him forever. Orfeo is resolved to make the attempt, but already he is apprehensive: how will Euridice feel when he refuses to look at her?

Act 2. begins at the fiery entrance to the underworld, where Furies and Spectres howl in unison a wild, fierce song (*Chi mai dell'Erebo – Who dares to come to the underworld*). Under the spell of Orfeo's music, however, the wild creatures gradually grow calmer and ask what his business is with them (*Misero giovine! Che vuoi, che mediti? – Wretched youth, what do you want? What do you plan?*). Reluctantly they permit the great door of the underworld to swing open on its black hinges, and Orfeo steps forward into the underworld.

Scene 2. takes place in the Elysian fields, the abode of the blessed dead.

Kathleen Ferrier (1912–1953), the famous English contralto, in a
1953 Covent Garden production of Gluck's *Orfeo*, her final role
before her death.

Its tranquility is underscored by a ballet of the Blessed Spirits, a haunting
flute solo, and finally a lyrical aria by Euridice (*Questo asilo di placide calme
– This refuge of quiet calm*). Orfeo enters, to be impressed with the still
beauty of the place (*Che puro ciel! Che chiaro sol! – How pure the sky! How
bright the sun!*), but he realizes that without Euridice he cannot be happy.
Finally, a group of Heroes and Heroines command Euridice to return to
Orfeo, telling her that she is fortunate to have found another paradise in
his love.

Act 3. takes place in a forest between the Elysian fields and earth.
Orfeo leads Euridice by the hand, urging her to follow him, but she
hesitates, wondering why he refuses to look at her, and laments that she
would prefer her peaceful death to the fear that Orfeo no longer loves her
(*Che fiero momento! – What a fearful moment!*). Finally Orfeo is overcome
and turns to her. With his promise broken, Euridice finds herself dying
once again. In a moving aria (*Che farò senza Euridice? – What will I do
without Euridice?*) Orfeo laments that no hope is left for him in heaven or
on earth and resolves to join his beloved in death. Yet all is not lost. Love

again enters, to tell Orfeo that he has proven his faith in spite of all, and that Euridice will be returned to him. A group of Heroes and Heroines arrive to join the happy couple in praising the god of love.

Orfeo ed Euridice was followed by another popular opera, *Alceste* (1767). However, Gluck seems to have had no immediate effect on the development of opera. It was only later, in the 19th century, that his ideas were to be followed up in the works of Berlioz.

18th-Century Comic Opera – Mozart

At the same time that Händel and later Gluck were devoting their energies to the composition of serious or tragic operas, a separate tradition of comic opera (*opera buffa, opéra comique* and *Singspiel*, in Italy, France and Germany, respectively) continued to grow and develop. Essentially a popular form, comic opera plots were light, situational comedies in which the action was far more important than expression of character or emotion. They were often performed by second-rate singers, or by actors who sang a little, and the music was consequently quite simple and very different from the elaborate style designed for the famous singers of *opera seria*. Except in the Italian *opera buffa*, spoken dialogue was the rule.

Opera buffa drew much of its inspiration from the *commedia dell'arte*, the improvised street plays of Italy. In the beginning, an *intermezzo* with characters drawn from the *commedia dell'arte* was performed in two sections between the three acts of an *opera seria*. One of the most famous of these, *La serva padrona* (*The Maid Turned Mistress*) – (1733), was written by Giovanni Battista Pergolesi (1710–1736). This witty tale of social classes turned topsy-turvy contains a variety of light music: quick, gay and vigorous arias, some slower songs of a more serious nature (often in jest), folk songs or songs in the popular idiom, and patter songs, in which fast moving repeated notes convey a great deal of text at high speed. *Secco* recitative is the common coinage, although *accompagnato* recitative is used in parody of *opera seria* for comic effect. Characteristic of the *intermezzo*, (and of its direct descendant, the *opera buffa*) is Pergolesi's use of the bass voice, which makes possible the ensembles that fall at the end of acts. At some point the *intermezzo* began to be performed as a unit after the *opera seria*, and eventually it was performed entirely separately. *Opera buffa* had come into its own.

Giovanni Paisiello (1740–1816) was an early master of *opera buffa*. His *Barbiere di Siviglia* (1782), based on the popular play by Beaumarchais, was so beloved by the public that when Rossini composed another setting of the play thirty-four years later it was considered to be extremely presumptuous on his part.

The parallel but separate traditions of *opera seria* and *opera buffa* were part of the musical environment of Wolfgang Amadeus Mozart (1756–1791), who composed six major operas in his short life. Mozart was born into a family of professional musicians in Salzburg, Austria, and throughout his childhood, he and his talented older sister, Marianne, toured Europe and performed in most of the major musical capitals. He was influenced in his operatic compositions not only by the traditions of *opera seria* and *opera buffa*, but also by the new instrumental forms which developed from the experiments of a group of musicians in Mannheim, Germany, led by the composer Johann Stamitz (1717–1757). This new approach to orchestral music took advantage of the orchestra's ability to play loudly or softly and to shift gradually from one extreme to the other. Mozart began to consider orchestration in terms of emotional expression for the characters of an opera, and he chose his instrumental colours to emphasize the dramatic action of the play. Mozart's orchestra produces a running commentary on the action – supporting it, doubting it or making fun of it. Mozart is also known for the great variety of forms to be found in his operas. Unlike earlier composers who relied on one or two standard forms (the *da capo* aria or the melodically repetitive verses of the folk song), Mozart presented his vocal material in forms deliberately chosen for maximum dramatic effect. An interest in extended harmonic forms is also evident in his operas, where large units are composed within the framework of specific carefully coordinated keys.

Following the *opera buffa* tradition of an individualistic interpretation of operatic characters, Mozart is concerned to present human beings in their complexity and changeability. His characters often do things for several different reasons at once, or try their best to deal with conflicting emotions. Another feature of Mozart's operas, also rooted in the *buffa* tradition, is his use of the ensemble. The earlier composers of *opera seria* had used the chorus to comment on the action of the opera, following the ancient tradition of the classical Greek and Roman playwrights. Even their duets and rare trios moulded the observations or emotions of the individual characters into a unified observation of a situation. While Mozart's ensembles occasionally serve this function, especially at the ends of acts, more often they pit groups of characters or individual characters against each other, highlighting individuality rather than submerging it. While the ensembles of earlier composers usually commented on completed actions, dramatic action of some importance to the plot often takes place during Mozart's.

Mozart began writing opera at the age of twelve with *La finta semplice* (*The Pretended Simpleton*), an *opera buffa*; and *Bastien und Bastienne*, a one-act operetta in German. *Idomeneo, rè di Creta* (*Idomeneo, King of Crete*) (1781), his first major opera, was an *opera seria* with many of the standard

Frederica von Stade, one of the most noted interpreters of the role of Cherubino, with Elizabeth Harwood as the Countess in a 1973 Glyndebourne production of *The Marriage of Figaro*.

features of the genre. *Die Entführung aus dem Serail* (*The Abduction from the Seraglio*), which follows the pattern of the German *Singspiel* (a spoken play with musical inserts), was first performed in Vienna in 1782. This opera remains in today's repertory.

On May 1, 1786, *Le nozze di Figaro* (*The Marriage of Figaro*) was first performed at the Burgtheater in Vienna. The libretto, written by Lorenzo da Ponte (1749–1838), was based on the second of three plays about the clever barber, Figaro, written by Pierre Augustin Caron de Beaumarchais (1732–1799). The first of the plays, *Le Barbier de Séville* (*The Barber of Seville*), had been set to music by the *buffa* composer Paisiello and had been wildly successful at its first performance in 1782. The second play, *Le Mariage de Figaro* (*The Marriage of Figaro*), had created a major public scandal when it was performed in Paris and had been banned by the censors in Vienna, where Mozart was working. Its depiction of clever servants and ridiculous masters caused the authorities to do more than raise their eyebrows. But set to music as an Italian opera, the play was passed by the censors, and the enthusiasm with which the

Cherubino (Sally Burgess) is discovered hiding in the chair as the Count (Christian du Plessis) makes love to Susanna (Lillian Watson). (English National Opera, 1978)

first performance was received fully justified Mozart's choice of subject.

In the *opera buffa* tradition, the female leads of *Le nozze di Figaro* are sung by women, not *castrati*, and the hero, Figaro, is sung by a baritone. Cherubino, the young page, is sung by a woman, beginning a long tradition of 'pants parts' (the part of a boy or young man usually sung by a female mezzo-soprano).

The overture is often performed as a concert piece. It reflects the light character of the play to follow, with some hints of serious overtones conveyed by short ventures into the minor key. The action of the opera is set in the palace of Count Almaviva near Seville in the 17th century.

Act 1. takes place in a room which is soon to be occupied by Figaro and his wife-to-be, the maid Susanna. Figaro is measuring the room (*Cinque, dieci, venti, trento – Five, ten, twenty, thirty*) to see if the Count's wedding gift of a bed will fit, while Susanna is trying on her wedding cap. The two disagree about the suitability of the room. Figaro feels that its close proximity to the quarters of their master and mistress is an advantage until Susanna reveals that the Count wants to pursue his traditional prerogative as lord of the manor and intends to sleep with her before she is married to Figaro. The Countess rings, and Susanna leaves Figaro to vow sarcastically that he will foil the Count's plans (*Se vuol' ballare, Signor Contino* – *If you want to dance, my lord Count*).

Dr Bartolo and Marcellina (respectively the guardian and the chaperon of the Countess before her marriage) enter. Poor Figaro has promised to wed Marcellina if he cannot pay back some money that he owes her, and Bartolo now sings that he will defeat Figaro's plans to escape his fate (*La vendetta* – *Revenge*). As he leaves, Susanna enters and exchanges polite insults with Marcellina (*Via resti servita* – *Go ahead, I'm your servant*), who is defeated by Susanna's wit and also withdraws. Cherubino, the page, arrives to tell Susanna of his sad fate: the Count is sending him away to the army because he was discovered embracing Barbarina, the gardener's daughter. Nonetheless, Cherubino's real idol is the Countess, and with the high spirits of youth, he sings an amorous song to women and to love in general (*Non so più cosa son* – *I don't know anymore what I am*). He hides behind a chair as the Count enters to reveal to Susanna that he has been appointed ambassador to London and is taking her and Figaro with him. Just as he asks her to meet him alone in the garden that evening, Basilio, the music master, enters. The Count hides behind the chair as Cherubino slips into the front of it and is covered up by Susanna. When Basilio tells Susanna that the Count loves her, she orders him to leave. Slyly he insinuates that she loves Cherubino instead, which so annoys the Count that he comes out of hiding (*Cosa sento* – *What's this I hear?*). Susanna pretends to faint, thus frightening the men into trying to soothe her. Still annoyed, the Count declares that Cherubino must leave at once. He describes how he lifted the tablecloth in Barbarina's room and discovered him in hiding. Demonstrating this by lifting the chair cover, he is outraged to find Cherubino yet again. Fortunately for all, the embarrassing situation is interrupted by a procession of peasant youths who enter scattering flowers. Figaro asks the Count to place Susanna's wedding veil on her head as an indication that he renounces all rights to her. The Count cannot publicly deny the request, but he does achieve a postponement of the ceremony until later. Cherubino begs the Count not to send him away, but with no success. The Count leaves with Basilio, and Figaro is left to console Cherubino in the mock heroic aria 'Non più andrai': no longer will Cherubino be slipping into ladies' chambers, for now he's marching off to military glory. And together they march off the stage, with Susanna joining them.

Act 2. takes place in the Countess' apartments in the palace. Alone, the Countess laments in a poignant yet dignified aria that the Count no longer loves her (*Porgi, Amor* – *Grant, O Love*), and Susanna enters to sympathize. Then Figaro comes with astounding news: the Count will enforce his marriage to Marcellina if Figaro does not give him his way with Susanna. Figaro has a scheme, however. Susanna is to agree to meet the Count in the garden that evening, but she will be replaced at the meeting by Cherubino in woman's dress.

Cherubino enters, and the ladies beg him to sing the little song that he has written for the Countess (*Voi che sapete — You who know*). After locking the door, they begin to dress him, coming across his commission to the regiment in the process. It had been issued in such a hurry that it lacks the official seal. They have just finished costuming him when the Count knocks on the door. The Countess, fearing his jealousy, maintains that she is alone in the room. Cherubino is quickly locked in the Countess' closet, and Susanna retreats to the adjoining room. When the Count enters, already suspicious, there is a loud crash inside the closet. Angrily he demands to know who is there, as Susanna slips back in from the other room and hides. Told that it is only Susanna, the Count goes away in disbelief to get tools to break the closet lock, taking the Countess with him and locking her bedroom door behind them. Susanna lets Cherubino out of the closet, and he, seeing no other escape, jumps out the window. Then she conceals herself in the closet to await the Count's return. In despair the Countess confesses that it is Cherubino in the closet and tries to explain, but the Count will not listen. He takes the key from her and opens the door . . . to reveal Susanna! The Count can only beg forgiveness in amazement. At once another complication arises. Figaro enters to announce that the musicians have arrived for the wedding. He is interrupted by Antonio, the gardener, who claims that a man was thrown from the Countess' balcony into the garden. At first Figaro tries to convince the Count that Antonio is drunk. Then he confesses that it was he who jumped from the balcony. The gardener offers to return the papers which he lost as he jumped. Figaro is perplexed: what papers? But with the aid of Susanna and the Countess, he is able to conclude that Antonio is referring to Cherubino's commission and to say that the page gave it to him because it lacked . . . ah yes, the seal! Having escaped one trap, Figaro falls into another, for Marcellina, Bartolo and Basilio enter, demanding that Figaro marry Marcellina at once. The final ensemble presents the viewpoints of all concerned.

Act 3. takes place in a drawing room where the wedding is to take place. The Count is joined by Susanna, who tells him that she will meet him in the garden that evening after all. In duet (*Crudel! Perchè finor — Cruel one! Why until now*) she reassures him that she will not fail to come. As she leaves, she runs into Figaro and tells him that their case is won. Overhearing her, the Count falls to wondering what trickery is afoot (*Vedro mentr'io sospiro — Shall I see while I live*) and vows vengeance on

Figaro. Don Curzio, a stammering lawyer (a stock character from the *buffa* tradition), enters with Marcellina, Bartolo and Figaro. When ordered to marry Marcellina, Figaro says he cannot do so without the consent of his parents (who are of noble birth!). He was kidnapped as a child, and although he can prove his birth by the possession of a certain birthmark, he has no papers. At this Marcellina suddenly recognizes him as her and Bartolo's long lost illegitimate son. Susanna enters, intending to tell Figaro that she can now pay off Marcellina with her dowry from the Count, and is infuriated to find him embracing her rival. After everything is explained, all exit to arrange a double wedding ceremony.

Barbarina and Cherubino make plans to disguise Cherubino as a girl so that he may join a procession to present flowers to the Countess. The Countess enters alone, sadly remembering the days when the Count loved her and hoping that someday he may love her again (*Dove sono – Where are the days*). She leaves as the Count enters with Antonio, who reveals that Cherubino has not gone to Seville but remains in the area dressed as a woman. Following close on this interchange, Susanna arrives to write, with the Countess' assistance, a letter to the Count, setting a meeting place for the evening (*Che soave zeffiretto – What a gentle breeze*). Barbarina enters with the other girls and her 'cousin' – actually Cherubino – who is undiscovered until Antonio and the Count come to look for him. In his final attempt to get rid of the page, the Count is stymied by Barbarina, who insists that she wants to marry him. Marcellina and Bartolo join Susanna and Figaro in kneeling before the Count to receive a wedding blessing. As they kneel, Susanna is able to hand the Count her letter, sealed with a pin.

Act 4. takes place in the garden later in the evening. Barbarina enters with a lantern, searching for something she has lost (*L'ho perduta – I have lost it*). When Figaro arrives, she tells him that she was to return a pin to Susanna from the Count, but she has lost it. Figaro immediately jumps to the conclusion that Susanna is deceiving him and learns where she is to meet the Count. He arranges that Bartolo and Basilio shall act as witnesses of Susanna's unfaithfulness and falls to lamenting his betrayal (*Aprite un po' quegl' occhi – Open your eyes for awhile*). He hides as Susanna, the Countess and Marcellina enter. Realizing that Figaro is watching, and deciding to tease him, Susanna sings a love song (*Deh vieni, non tardar – Then come, do not tarry*), which Figaro assumes to be directed to the Count. The Countess and Susanna then exchange clothing, and when the Count arrives, he begins to make love to his wife (whom he believes to be Susanna), giving her a ring as a pledge. Figaro, running into Susanna (whom he believes to be the Countess), tells her that they now can trap Susanna and the Count. When he suddenly realizes that she is not the Countess, he cannot resist teasing her by declaring his passion for her.

Don Giovanni's greatest mistake was to mock the statue of the man whom he killed. (English National Opera)

Angrily she slaps him, but Figaro is able to convince her that he knew who she was all along. The Count enters, looking for 'Susanna', who has wandered off, only to find Figaro kneeling before the 'Countess'. Figaro is caught by the Count, who calls at once for his servants, who arrive followed by Antonio, Basilio and Bartolo. Reaching into the arbour, where he believes the 'Countess' to be hiding, the Count pulls out Cherubino, Barbarina, Marcellina and finally Susanna, dressed as the 'Countess'. Susanna kneels at the Count's feet, asking forgiveness, which the Count refuses. Only when the Countess, still dressed as Susanna, arrives, does the Count realize that he has lost the game. Humbly he asks for forgiveness, which the Countess grants. All rejoice at the happy ending.

Only a year later Mozart produced another successful opera, *Don Giovanni* (*Don Juan*), which was first performed at the National Theatre in Prague on October 29, 1787. Its libretto was written by da Ponte (the writer of the libretto for *Figaro*), who took much of his material from a libretto written in 1775 by Giovanni Bertati.

The story, which has a long pedigree in European folklore and drama, tells of a certain Don Juan who is known for his enormous success with the ladies (2,065 conquests, all told!). Unfortunately he makes the mistake of killing the father of one of his attempted conquests, and the girl seeks to avenge her father with the assistance of her fiancé and another abandoned mistress of Don Juan. Finally Don Juan commits the ultimate sacrilege of laughing at the dead and inviting the statue of the murdered father (the *commendatore*) to dinner. The statue accepts, arrives at Don Juan's house, and drags him, still unrepentant, down to Hell.

This opera was followed by *Così fan tutte* (*Thus do All Women*), a comic opera dealing with the fickleness of women in love, which was premièred in 1790, and by *La clemenza di Tito* (*The Clemency of Titus*), an *opera seria*, which was written in 18 days for the coronation festivities of Leopold II of Bohemia in 1791.

In May, 1791, Mozart received an invitation to compose an opera from a friend of his, an actor and theatre manager named Emanuel Schikaneder. Mozart accepted the offer, perhaps out of friendship for Schikaneder, who, like Mozart, was a Freemason. (At this time Freemasonry was a strongly ideological movement, widely opposed by both church and state as a threat to the existing social system, and the brotherhood of Masons was extremely close.) The result of their collaboration was *Die Zauberflöte* (*The Magic Flute*).

The Viennese public of the day was showing a great interest in fairytale operas set in romantic and exotic locales. Schikaneder found a suitable story in '*Lulu, oder die Zauberflöte*' ('Lulu, or the Magic Flute'), by A. J. Liebeskind, which had been published with a group of Oriental fairytales in 1786. He wrote a libretto for a traditional German *Singspiel* with spoken dialogue, and Mozart set to work on the music. A month later another opera based on the very same story, *Der Fagottist, oder die Zauberzither*, was premièred at the theatre of Schikaneder's arch-rival in Vienna. This made necessary a reworking of *Die Zauberflöte*'s plot. The locale was switched from the Orient to Egypt, and the relationship of the characters was altered. The story begins with a good queen and a wicked magician, but halfway through the opera their roles are reversed, and the queen becomes the agent of evil and the magician the agent of good. At the same time, the fairytale was twisted to form an allegory of Freemasonry. The secret brotherhood of initiates, the idea of enlightenment through ritual ordeals, the interest in ancient Egyptian religion – all suggest Masonic teachings and practices.

The overture, which is often performed as a concert piece, emphasizes the number three by its presentation of three punctuated chords, which are heard again during the Act 2. temple scene. Three, an important number for the Freemasons, is certainly the magic number of this opera – three youths, three ladies, three trials, three temples and so on.

Act 1. begins in a rocky wilderness near the Temple of Isis. Tamino, a prince, enters, pursued by an enormous serpent. Finding that he has no more arrows with which to defend himself, he begs the gods for mercy and then faints (*Zu Hilfe! Zu Hilfe! – Help! Help!*). As he does so, the temple door opens and three veiled ladies carrying silver spears rush to his aid and kill the serpent. Then they fall to discussing his good looks (*Sie ist vollbracht, die Heldentat! – The heroic act is done*). After an argument about which of them should remain with him, they all leave to tell the Queen what has happened.

Tamino awakes and sees the dead serpent. He hides as the irrepressible Papageno comes in carrying an enormous cage of birds. Dressed like a brightly coloured bird himself, he carries in his hands a Pan's pipe with which he makes a five-note bird-like call. He introduces himself in an infectious folk-like aria (*Der Vogelfänger bin ich ja – I am the birdcatcher*), telling us that what he really wants is a wife. When Tamino comes out of hiding, Papageno boasts untruthfully that it was he who killed the serpent. The three ladies return briefly, to punish Papageno for his lie by locking his mouth with a golden padlock and to present Tamino with a portrait of the Queen's lovely daughter Pamina. Alone, Tamino meditates on her exceptional beauty (*Dies Bildnis ist bezaubernd schön – This image is magically fair*), realizing that he has found love. The three ladies appear yet again to tell him that the Queen is willing to aid him in his suit if he will rescue her daughter from the wicked sorcerer who has carried her off. As Tamino agrees, a clap of thunder introduces the Queen of the Night. She does not descend to spoken dialogue like the rest of the characters. In recitative she tells Tamino that she does not fear for his success, and then, in a coloratura aria straight from the *seria* tradition (*Zum Leiden bin ich auserkoren – I have been chosen to suffer*), she tells of her daughter's abduction and promises that if Tamino will save her, she shall be his bride. Without further discussion she and the three ladies vanish.

Tamino, unsure whether he has dreamed the whole thing, again encounters Papageno, who can only hum, since his mouth has been padlocked. Luckily the three ladies return to free him, and they also give Tamino a magic flute from the Queen, which will protect him in danger. Papageno is assigned to Tamino as his servant for the trip to the kingdom of Sarastro (the wicked magician) and is given a set of silver bells for protection. The ladies leave, promising that three youths will appear to be their guides.

Scene 2. takes place in an elegant Egyptian room in Sarastro's palace.

Tamino (Thomas Round) charms the animals with his flute.
(Sadler's Wells, 1955)

Monostatos, Sarastro's uncouth Moorish servant, threatens the captive Pamina with death. Papageno enters and recognizes Pamina, but he is terrified by Monostatos and runs away. Monostatos, in turn, is terrified by Papageno's strange appearance and runs in the other direction. Papageno returns to tell Pamina that he has been sent to help rescue her and to take her to Tamino. Sadly he says that he would like to have a wife too, and together they sing a duet (*Bei Männern, welche Liebe fühlen – All men who feel love*) praising the noble power of love.

Scene 3. takes place in a grove in front of three temples: the Temple of Nature, the Temple of Reason and the Temple of Wisdom. The three youths (often sung by three boys) advise Tamino to be steadfast, patient and silent (*Zum Ziele führt dich diese Bahn – This path leads to your goal*). Tamino tries to enter the Temple of Reason and the Temple of Nature, but voices call out to him to stand back. When he tries to enter the Temple of Wisdom, an old priest appears with a word of warning: only when friendship and love lead him into the Brotherhood will he learn where Pamina is and what Sarastro's motives were in kidnapping her. The priest returns into the Temple, and a chorus of priests from within assures Tamino that Pamina lives. In joy he plays his magic flute, and at once he is surrounded by animals who are charmed by his music, but Pamina does not appear. Then he hears Papageno's pipes and hurries off to find him.

Pamina and Papageno enter, fleeing from Monostatos and looking for Tamino (*Schnelle Füsse, rascher Mut – Swift feet, rash courage*). Even as they hear Tamino's flute, Monostatos appears. Quickly Papageno plays his magic bells. Monostatos and his slaves fall into a trance, singing and dancing away (*Das klinget so herrlich – That rings so gloriously*).

A procession now enters, followed by Sarastro. Pamina kneels, confessing that she had attempted to flee, and is forgiven. When Tamino is dragged in by Monostatos, the two lovers recognize each other and joyfully embrace. Monostatos, hoping for a reward, tells Sarastro that he caught Tamino trying to abduct Pamina, but Sarastro, knowing the truth, sends him out to be punished. Then Tamino and Pamina are led away to the Temple.

Act 2. begins in a grove of palms. Sarastro enters with the priests, whom he informs of Tamino's search for enlightenment. The three chords of the overture are heard again, and Sarastro explains that Tamino and Pamina are destined for each other. For this reason he took her from her mother, who is trying to destroy the Temple of the priests. He then asks them to accept Tamino and Papageno into the Temple and prays to the gods to endow them with wisdom and patience in their forthcoming ordeals (*O Isis und Osiris – O Isis and Osiris*).

Scene 2. takes place in front of the Temple at night. The Speaker arrives with the priests. Tamino boldly says that he is ready to face the first ordeal, but Papageno tells them that actually all he wants is food, drink, sleep and a wife. He is told that Sarastro had planned a companion for him, but that he may not speak to her during the ordeal, just as Tamino may not speak to Pamina.

Alone again, the two are visited by the three ladies, who try unsuccessfully to pursuade them to flee (*Ihr an diesem Schreckensort? – Are you in this dreadful place?*). The Speaker and the priests return to congratulate Tamino on surviving this trial and lead him and Papageno away to the next ordeal.

Scene 3. takes place in a garden of Sarastro's palace, where Pamina is asleep in the moonlight. Monostatos creeps in, planning to steal a kiss (*Alles fühlt der Liebe Freuden – Everyone may feel the joys of love*), but as he moves close to Pamina a clap of thunder introduces the Queen of the Night, and he slinks off in terror. Pamina implores her mother to take her home, but instead the Queen gives her a dagger, so that she may kill Sarastro and repossess the shield of the sun, without which the Queen is powerless. In a brilliant coloratura aria (*Der Hölle Rache kocht in meinem Herzen – The vengeance of Hell burns in my heart*) she threatens to disown Pamina if she is unsuccessful in this task. Next Pamina is accosted by Monostatos, who threatens to kill her, but fortunately Sarastro enters to send him away. Unhappy, Pamina pleads with him to spare her mother, and Sarastro replies that her revenge is unknown (*In diesen heil'gen Hallen – In these hallowed halls*).

Scene 4. takes place in a large hall. Tamino and Papageno are led in by the Speaker and the priests, who remind them of their vow of silence and leave. An old crone brings a cup of water to the thirsty Papageno and declares that she is his true love. She is followed by the three youths, who enter briefly with food, drink, the flute and the bells (*Seid uns zum zweitenmal willkommen – We welcome you a second time*). Pamina comes when she hears Tamino's flute, but neither he nor Papageno will speak to her. Brokenhearted, she laments that she is no longer loved (*Ach, ich fühl's, es ist verschwunden – Ah, I know that it is gone*) and sadly leaves.

Scene 5. takes place in the vault below the Temple. Led by Sarastro (*O Isis und Osiris – O Isis and Osiris*), the priests rejoice that Tamino will soon be worthy to join them. Tamino is then led in to bid farewell to Pamina before he undergoes two further trials.

After the priests and Tamino leave, Papageno enters. The Speaker tells him that he really should be punished for breaking his vow of silence, but that the merciful gods will spare him, although he will never share in the joys of the elect. Characteristically undismayed, he sings, accompanying himself on his bells, of his desire for a wife (*Ein Mädchen oder Weibchen – a little maid or little wife*). At the end of his song the old crone enters and

Papageno (Geraint Evans) prepares to hang himself when
Papagena fails to appear. (Covent Garden, 1961)

---

promises to love him if he will be faithful to her. Papageno swears that he
will (conditionally), upon which she turns into the young girl, Papagena.
Before he can reach out to her, however, the Speaker returns to tell him
that he is not yet worthy and takes Papagena away.

Scene 6. takes place in a garden near the Temple. The three youths
enter singing a hymn to the sun (*Bald prangt, den Morgen zu verkünden* –
Soon the morning will shine) and notice that Pamina is about to kill herself
with the dagger. Reassuring her that Tamino still loves her, they promise
to take her to him.

Scene 7. takes place in the mountains in front of two enormous gates.
Tamino is brought in by the priests, who sing of conquering the fear of
death (*Der, welcher wandert diese Strasse* – *He who wanders this path*).
Tamino says that he does not fear death, but will follow the path of
virtue. Pamina then joins Tamino, and as he plays his magic flute, they
enter the gates to pass through trial by fire and water.

Scene 8. takes place in a garden. Papageno comes in calling for
Papagena with his Pan's pipes. When she does not come, he slowly
prepares to hang himself but is rescued by the three youths, who advise

56

him to play his bells. He does, and Papagena arrives. Together they plan to have a whole family of little Papagenos and Papagenas.

Scene 9. takes place in darkness in front of the Temple. The Queen and her ladies creep in, led by Monostatos. Suddenly they are destroyed with a clap of thunder and the scene is brilliant with light. In Scene 10. Sarastro appears with Tamino and Pamina to proclaim that with their success light has conquered darkness. All join in a hymn of praise to the two lovers (*Heil sei euch Geweihten! – Hail to you, O initiates*).

Die Zauberflöte was not terribly successful at first, but Schikaneder persevered in presenting it, perhaps because he was a friend of Mozart, or perhaps because the role of Papageno, which he himself played, pleased him very much. At his theatre alone, the work had 223 performances by 1851, and it soon became one of the world's most popular operas.

The Turn of the Century – Cherubini, Spontini and Beethoven

After the death of Mozart in 1791, leadership in opera composition was assumed by Paris, or, more precisely, by the Paris Opéra. It maintained this ascendancy for more than half a century, and even the greatest of later nineteenth-century composers, Wagner and Verdi, would not feel that they had received the seal of success until one of their operas was performed in Paris.

An interest in classical subjects (ancient mythology and history) survived the French Revolution (1789), and two Italian composers, writing in French in Paris, found that operas with classical themes were very popular. Luigi Cherubini (1760–1842) is remembered especially for his opera *Médée* (*Medea*–1797), and Gasparo Spontini (1774–1851), Napoleon's favorite composer, is known for *La Vestale* (*The Vestal Virgin*–1807). Both of these composers specialized in the 'rescue opera', a popular form of the time. The plots of this type of opera revolve around the sacrifices and loyalty of a lover or friend who rescues the beloved from some pressing danger. No doubt the violence of the French Revolution, in which such escapes were commonplace, stimulated interest in this suspense form.

The classic rescue opera is *Fidelio* by Ludwig van Beethoven (1770–1827). First performed at the Theater an der Wien, in Vienna, in 1805, Beethoven's only opera was the result of years of searching for a libretto that satisfied his qualifications. Beethoven refused on principle to accept any libretto dealing with magic or having even faint suggestions of immorality. He was, however, very impressed by Spontini's *La*

Vestale and by Cherubini's *Les Deux Journées* (*The Two Days*–1800), which, in addition to being a noted example of a rescue opera, placed great emphasis on the human values of loyalty, kindness and devotion. Eventually he found something suitable for reworking in an earlier libretto by Jean–Nicolas Bouilly, which had been performed in Paris in 1798 with music by Pierre Gaveau under the title *Léonore, ou l'amour conjugal* (*Leonora, or a wife's love*). Like many operas of the time, *Fidelio* drew criticism from the censors. In the wake of the French Revolution its portrayal of corrupt civil authorities was considered highly inflammatory, and performance was permitted only after certain revisions had been made. In any case the opera was not especially successful at its first performance and drew only a small audience in part because Napoleon's troops had taken Vienna only a week before the opening.

Fidelio, like *Zauberflöte*, is written in the form of a *Singspiel* (that is, with spoken dialogue). It was obviously difficult for Beethoven to write the lighter music required for the less serious characters of the piece, and his music often overwhelms their texts – to the great pleasure of the listener. Musically the work is closely related to Beethoven's Third Symphony, the *Eroica*, which was written just before he began work on *Fidelio*, and like the *Eroica*, *Fidelio* is dedicated to a portrait of heroism. It represents the triumph of idealistic political values and the fidelity of human love against a background of political squalor and corruption.

After its unsuccessful initial performance, Beethoven made several revisions, but it was only when a fourth version with considerable text changes was premièred in Vienna in 1814 at the Court Opera that the work finally achieved success. By this time Beethoven had composed four overtures for it. The last composed, 'Fidelio', which makes a smooth bridge to the beginning of the first act, is the one commonly played in that position, while 'Leonore No. 3' is usually played before the second scene of Act 2.

The opera takes place in eighteenth-century Seville. Florestan, a nobleman, has been imprisoned in an underground dungeon by Pizarro, the Governor of the prison of Seville and a political enemy. Although rumour says that Florestan is dead, his wife Leonora believes that he is still alive, and she has disguised herself as a young man, Fidelio, to try to free him. She is the assistant to Rocco, the jailer. Her position is made more difficult by the fact that Marcellina, daughter of Rocco, has fallen in love with her, a situation appreciated little by Rocco and not at all by Jaquino, Rocco's gatekeeper, who is himself in love with Marcellina.

Act 1. takes place in the courtyard of the prison. Near the gate is the house of Rocco and Marcellina and also the smaller house of Jaquino. While Marcellina irons clothes, Jaquino vainly tries to convince her to marry him (*Jetzt, Schätzchen – Now, little sweetheart*). When Jaquino is

The contralto Maria Malibran (1808–1836) was famous for her portrayal of Fidelio.

called away to attend the gate, she admits to herself that it is actually Fidelio whom she loves (*O wär ich schon mit dir vereint – If only I were married to you*). Jaquino returns with Rocco as Fidelio arrives, and in a beautiful quartet, written in the form of a canon or round, all present their own reflections on the proposed match (*Mir ist so wunderbar – It seems so miraculous*). When Jaquino leaves, Rocco tells Fidelio and Marcellina that he approves of their marriage, but he warns them, in an elegant aria in the *buffa* style, that they will also need money. (*Hat man nicht auch Gold beineben – If one has no gold on hand*).

Fidelio offers to assist Rocco with the prisoners who are kept in the underground dungeon. Rocco accepts his aid, but says that he cannot permit him to go to one particular cell, where a man has been held for more than two years and is being slowly starved to death. The following trio expresses Marcellina's joy at the proposed match, Fidelio's hope that her husband still lives, and Rocco's encouragement of Fidelio as a suitor.

Pizarro, the Governor, now arrives and receives from Rocco dispatches which contain a warning: Don Fernando, Prime Minister of

Spain, has heard that Pizarro is unjustly holding certain political prisoners and tomorrow there is to be a surprise investigation. In anger Pizarro decides to kill Florestan to avoid discovery (*Ha! welch' ein Augenblick! – Ha! what a moment!*).

Pizarro orders a watch to be kept to announce any visitors long in advance. He offers Rocco money to kill the prisoner, but when Rocco fearfully refuses he decides to do the deed himself. As both men leave, Fidelio, who has overheard them, at first despairs (*Abscheulicher! Wo eilst du hin? – Villain, where are you hurrying?*) but then finds hope and courage to make the attempt to save her husband (*Komm, Hoffnung – Come, hope*).

Marcellina, Jaquino and Rocco appear. Fidelio begs Rocco to allow the prisoners kept above ground to go into the garden, as surely the governor will not come at this hour. As they move into the unfamiliar sunlight the prisoners sing one of the most beautiful choruses in all opera (*O welche Lust – O what joy*), a moving hymn to freedom. Rocco tells Fidelio that Pizarro has not only sanctioned his marriage to Marcellina but has also given permission for Fidelio to assist with the underground prisoners. He confides that the starving prisoner will soon require a grave. Fidelio therefore must help him to open an old cistern in the dungeon for this purpose. Pizarro enters unexpectedly and, furious that the prisoners have been permitted into the garden, orders them back to their cells.

Act 2. begins in the underground prison where Florestan sings sorrowfully of his love for Leonora (*In des Lebens Frühlingstagen – In the springtime of life*). Deliriously he imagines that he sees her coming to lead him to heaven. Rocco enters with Fidelio to open the old cistern. In the dim light Fidelio cannot tell if the prisoner is in fact her husband until he speaks. A trio (*Euch werde Lohn in bessern Welten – You will be repaid in a better world*) follows in which Florestan wonders if he can enlist Fidelio's aid, while Rocco voices his sympathy and Fidelio prays for courage. Rocco then gives a prearranged signal to Pizarro, who enters in disguise. In the following quartet (*Er sterbe! – He shall die!*), a fiery dialogue takes place. Pizarro identifies himself to Florestan, who treats him with scorn. Fidelio throws herself between Pizarro's dagger and Florestan, identifying herself as Leonora as she points a gun at the Governor. A trumpet call is heard, announcing the arrival of the Prime Minister, and Jaquino comes to get Rocco and Pizarro. The two lovers remain and sing an exultant duet (*O namenlose Freude – O nameless joy*). As it ends, Leonora leads Florestan from his cell.

Scene 2. takes place in the parade grounds of the fortress. Don Fernando, Prime Minister of Spain, enters with his officers and Pizarro. From the opposite side the prisoners are led in by Jaquino and Marcellina. As the Prime Minister announces that he has come to bring justice, Rocco leads forward Leonora and Florestan. Don Fernando is astonished

Florestan (Hugh Beresford), imprisoned and prematurely old,
raises his hands in supplication as he catches sight of Leonora.

to see his friend, whom he believed to be dead. At once he orders Pizarro
to be led away and gives to Leonora the honour of unlocking her
husband's chains. In joy she and Florestan sing of the happiness of their
reunion, while the crowd praises Leonora's virtue and love.

Italian Opera at the Beginning of the 19th Century – Rossini

One of the most creative and influential of early 19th-century composers
was Gioacchino Antonio Rossini (1792–1868), who by the age of 37 had
produced fifteen successful operas. Many were written on historical or
classical subjects, following the French tradition, but only his last opera,

Guillaume Tell (*William Tell* – 1829) was premièred at the Paris Opéra.

Rossini is noted for strongly marked rhythmic motives and lively melodies which are composed of short phrases supported by a simple harmonic framework. He also developed a new group of musical forms which were imitated by the composers of the following generation. The most important of these was a new type of *scena*, which was built of two basic sections: (1) a long recitative followed by a slow aria section, called a *cavatina*, and (2) an optional section of recitative, perhaps punctuated by the chorus, followed by a fast aria section called a *cabaletta*, which was designed to show off a singer's voice. In hopes that the temperamental singers of his day would perform his music the way he wanted it, Rossini often wrote out the ornaments for this section. He also developed a new form for duets: (1) an introductory recitative, followed by a slow section in parallel thirds, sixths or tenths, and (2) a transitional section of recitative, possibly indicated by a dramatic interruption of the plot, followed by a faster section in which the voices sing the same melody one after the other. At the end the melody may be repeated once more in unison or in octaves. Rossini was also noted for his end-of-act ensembles in which everyone complains about the noise made by the other characters. The 'Rossini *crescendo*' helps to build excitement by repeating a phrase of music at successively higher pitches supported by increasingly heavy orchestration.

Rossini's best known opera is *Il barbiere di Siviglia* (*The Barber of Seville*), which is in many ways the summation of all that was delightful in Italian *opera buffa* at the turn of the century. *Il barbiere* is based on the first of the trilogy of plays written by Beaumarchais about the clever barber Figaro. Thirty-four years earlier, in 1783, the play had been set to music by Giovanni Paisiello (1740–1816) – a popular opera by one of the most popular opera composers of the previous generation. In need of an opera for immediate performance (it is said that *Il barbiere* was composed in thirteen days), Rossini decided to reset the play with a new libretto by Cesare Sterbini. As Paisiello's version was still extremely popular, Rossini found it necessary to take certain placatory measures, such as requesting permission of Paisiello to recompose the work. Despite this precaution, the première of *Il barbiere* at the Teatro Argentina in Rome on February 20, 1816, was a dismal failure, for the noise contributed by the partisan audience almost entirely drowned out the performance. Shortly thereafter, however, it won public acceptance and has remained in the repertory until the present day. It is interesting to note that the part of Rosina was initially written for a mezzo-soprano and only became a high soprano part when Jenny Lind, the 'Swedish Nightingale', raised the pitch of the famous aria '*Una voce poco fa*'. The overture is taken from an earlier opera by Rossini, *Aureliano in Palmira* (1813).

Jenny Lind (1820–1887), the Swedish soprano who was considered one of the most glamorous *prima donnas* of the 19th century.

Act 1. takes place outside the house of Dr Bartolo on a street in 17th-century Seville, just before dawn. Count Almaviva has arranged a serenade for Rosina, the ward of Dr Bartolo (*Ecco ridente in cielo – Behold, bright in the sky*), but Rosina does not appear. Disappointed, the Count pays off the musicians, who noisily disappear. The barber Figaro strolls in bragging that he is the busiest and cleverest man in town (*Largo al factotum della città – Easily the city's factotum*). He is the chief matchmaker of Seville, working with a razor by day and a guitar by night. He recognizes Almaviva, who begs him to keep his identity a secret and also reveals to him his love for Rosina. Figaro tells him that he is barber, hairdresser and general confidant to Bartolo's household, and is therefore in an ideal position to assist the Count. Suddenly Rosina appears on the balcony with a letter in her hand. In answer to a question from Bartolo, she says that she is holding the words for an aria from the opera *L'Inutil Precauzione* (*The Useless Precaution*). Seeing the Count in the street, she drops the letter, begging Bartolo to retrieve it for her. While he descends to the street, she has her chance to talk to the Count and agrees to run away with him, if he can find a way to arrange it. In an aside Figaro

63

tells the Count that Bartolo is planning to marry Rosina, who is an heiress, for her money. The Count again sings to her of his love (*Se il mio nome – If my name*), identifying himself as 'Lindoro', for he wants to be sure that she will love him and not his rank. Rosina is only able to tell him that she returns his affection before she has to go back inside the house.

Encouraged, the Count offers to pay Figaro for his assistance, to which Figaro responds that gold is above all what causes his great brain to work well (*All' idea di quel metallo – The thought of that money*). His plan is to get the Count into Bartolo's house disguised as a soldier assigned to lodge there. After a duet (*Che invenzione prelibata – What an ingenious invention*) in praise of Figaro's cleverness, Figaro tells the Count how to find his place of business (*Numero quindici – Number 15*). In a final duet (*Ah, che d'amore la fiamma io sento – Ah, how I feel the flame of love*), the Count expresses his hope that his courtship will be successful, while Figaro rejoices in the money he will surely receive.

Act 2. takes place in the drawing-room of Dr Bartolo's house. In an aria famous for its vocal pyrotechnics, Rosina sings of her determination to outwit her guardian and marry Lindoro (*Una voce poco fa – A voice a few moments ago*). As Figaro enters, she considers giving him her letter for Lindoro, but they are interrupted by Bartolo, who is very annoyed with Figaro. He has given the wrong medicines to the servants [a barber in those days was often also a doctor]: Ambrogio is drowsy because of a sleeping potion and Berta cannot stop sneezing because of a sneezing powder. Don Basilio, a music teacher and matchmaker, arrives to learn that Bartolo plans to marry Rosina at once. Basilio has discovered that Rosina's admirer is Count Almaviva and suggests that they can get rid of him by starting an unsavoury rumour about him (*La calunnia è un venticello – Slander is a little breeze*). Unimpressed, Bartolo demands that Basilio come to his room at once to draw up the marriage contract. Figaro meets Rosina to tell her that his cousin Lindoro, a hardworking student, is deeply in love with her. If she will but send him a letter as a token of her affection, he will come to the house. After Figaro leaves, Bartolo suggests suspiciously that she has written a letter, but she denies it. In an angry aria (*A un dottor della mia sorte – To a doctor of my sort*), he warns her that she cannot fool him and that she may expect to be more closely watched in the future. At this, Berta, still sneezing, shows in the Count, who is playing the role of a drunken soldier. While Bartolo searches for his exemption from accepting a billet, Rosina and the Count converse in asides. She cleverly conceals the transfer of her letter by dropping a laundry list, which is pounced upon by Bartolo. To add to the commotion, Berta and Basilio join them. Then Figaro arrives to say that a crowd has gathered in the street because of the noise. A sergeant arrives with his guards to remove the Count, but leaves when shown a paper

The music lesson scene from the 1966 Sadler's Wells Opera
revival of *The Barber of Seville*. Left to right: Almaviva (Louis
Browne), Rosina (Patricia Kern), Basilio (Noel Mangin), Marcellina
(Anna Cooper) and Bartolo (Denis Dowling).

revealing Almaviva's rank. The act ends in dramatic confusion and
musical uproar.

Act 3. takes place in the same room as Act 2. While Bartolo speculates
on the identity of the drunken soldier, the Count enters in a new disguise:
this time he is Don Alonzo, a substitute music teacher for Don Basilio,
who is (supposedly) ill. Bartolo fetches Rosina, who manages to converse with the Count during her lesson. She sings her aria from *L'Inutil
Precauzione* [many famous singers have substituted a favourite aria of
their own at this point], but Bartolo is displeased with it and suggests
another song, which he ends by singing himself (*Quando mi sei vicina* –
When you are near me). Figaro then enters to shave Bartolo, who at first
exits to get towels, but then, unwilling to leave Rosina unchaperoned,
hands his keys to Figaro instead. Having caused a distraction by breaking
some china in the hallway, Figaro is able to steal the key that opens the
door from the balcony into the house. As Figaro begins to shave Bartolo,
Basilio arrives, but the conspirators are able to convince him that he is ill
and should go home. A chance remark by the Count reawakens

Bartolo's suspicions, and he goes off to find Basilio. The two men return, having discovered that Basilio has never seen Don Alonzo in his life. Bartolo demands that Basilio bring a notary to him at once to arrange the marriage contract, but this proves impossible because the notary is, at that very moment, arranging a marriage contract for Figaro's niece. Thoroughly incensed, Bartolo calls Rosina and manages to convince her that 'Don Alonzo' and Figaro are plotting to marry her to Count Almaviva. Feeling betrayed, she reveals that Figaro has filched the balcony key. Together they plot to capture the pair, and she agrees to marry Bartolo at once. An orchestral interlude representing a storm follows, after which Figaro and the Count enter from the balcony. Rosina at first receives Lindoro with scorn but is pacified when she finds out that he is Count Almaviva himself. As Figaro tries to hurry them along, they exchange affectionate remarks. When they finally do decide to leave, they find that the ladder to the balcony has been removed and that two men are guarding the front door. The Count and Rosina hide as Basilio enters with the notary. Figaro asks him if he has prepared the contract for his 'niece' and then terrifies and bribes Basilio into witnessing the signatures of Rosina and the Count. Just then Bartolo enters with the sergeant and his guards and orders him to arrest the Count. Almaviva reveals his true identity and also the marriage contract and rejoices that he has at last freed Rosina from tyranny (*Cessa di più resistere* – *Don't resist any more*). Bartolo is somewhat cheered when he is told that he may keep Rosina's dowry, and all join with the chorus in rejoicing over the happy turn of events.

The Beginnings of German Romantic Opera – Weber

German romantic opera at the beginning of the 19th century represented a world outside the French or Italian orbit. Here there was a great interest in fairytales and legends, in stories set in distant and romantic lands, and in folk music. E. T. A. Hoffmann (1776–1822) was one of the most persuasive advocates of this concept of art, and he himself demonstrated it in his own poetry, music and essays. His opera *Undine* (1816) is generally considered to be the first romantic opera.

Carl Maria von Weber (1786–1826) achieved the musical success that Hoffmann did not. He had theatre in his blood, for his father was the director of a theatre, and he himself worked as an impresario and conductor at Breslau and Prague. His early operas, *Das Waldmädchen* (*The Woodland Maid* – 1800), *Peter Schmoll* (1803) and *Abu Hassan* (1811) were not notably successful, and it was only with the publication of a group of songs with texts by Theodor Körner (*Leyer und Schwert, Lyre and Sword* –

1814) that he achieved fame. In 1817 he began work on *Der Freischütz* (*The Freeshooter*, or *The Marksman*). A friend of his, Friedrich Kind (1768–1843), wrote the libretto, basing it on a story by Johann August Apel which had been published at Leipzig in 1810.

The story of the Freeshooter was based on the legend that a marksman could secure from the Devil (the Black Huntsman) seven magic bullets (called free bullets) in return for his soul at the end of a set period of time. Six of the bullets struck according to the will of the marksman; the seventh went where the Devil chose. The only way the contract could be extended was to supply the Devil with a substitute soul.

The ominous forest setting of *Der Freischütz* is notably different from the idealized and pastoral settings of Italian or French libretti of the period. The acceptance of a primitive past which influences or interprets the present was to become a major characteristic of German romantic opera. Weber's music, with its overtones of German folk song, is strikingly different from the sophisticated tunes of the Italian and French composers whose works dominated Germany at this time.

The opera is cast in the form of a *Singspiel* (an opera with spoken dialogue). Other elements of *Der Freischütz* which are characteristic of this form are the blameless heroine, the well-intentioned but incompetent hero, and the rustic village setting. First performed at the Schauspielhaus in Berlin on June 18, 1821, the opera was an immense and immediate success and appeared at once throughout Germany.

The overture, one of the most dazzling in all opera, presents many of the themes of the work to follow. After an opening horn melody evocative of the hunt, the themes of the Black Huntsman, the Wolf Glen, and Agathe's aria from Act 2. are heard.

The first act takes place in front of a rustic tavern in the forest. Max, a forester, is sitting alone at a table with a mug of beer, while a crowd watches Kilian, a young peasant, shoot the last star off a target. A procession is formed to honour him, and the participants make fun of Max, who has missed with every shot, as they pass his table. Kilian joins them in jeering (*Schau der Herr mich als König* – *Mister, look at me as king*), which impels Max to jump up and attack him. The fight is interrupted by Kuno, Kaspar and a group of huntsmen. Kaspar, who has already made a deal with Samiel, the Black Huntsman, suggests to Max that he should also obtain some free-bullets, while Kuno warns Max that if he fails in the trial shot on the following morning he will not be allowed to marry Kuno's daughter Agathe. Kuno then explains the origin of the trial shot: in the time of an ancestor of his, a gamekeeper also named Kuno, it was the custom to punish a poacher by tying him to a stag who was then released to be pursued by dogs. The prince of the time was roused to pity by this sight and promised the hereditary post of ranger to anyone who could kill the stag without wounding the thief. Kuno at once took aim and killed the stag. A man who was jealous of Kuno's success told the prince that Kuno had used a free-bullet. For this reason the prince made the office conditional on a demonstration of marksmanship by Kuno and each of his successors. In the following trio (*Oh, diese Sonne – Oh, this sun*), Kaspar tries again to interest Max in obtaining free-bullets, Max sings that he will never be able to renounce Agathe, and Kuno tries to be encouraging. Kuno, Kaspar and the huntsmen leave, as Kilian suggests a dance (a Bohemian waltz). As darkness falls, the dancers disappear into the tavern or the woods, and Max is left alone to sing sadly of the past in which he was able to go hunting with a light heart and to return at night to Agathe with a good catch (*Durch die Wälder – Through the woods*). Kaspar returns and offers Max a drink, into which he slips a drug. He finally succeeds in getting him to drink this by proposing a whole series of toasts. As the clock strikes seven, Max prepares to leave to visit Agathe, but he is detained by Kaspar who suggests that he can help him win the trial shot. He lends Max his gun, with which Max is able to shoot an eagle far out of normal range. Kaspar informs Max that the secret is a 'free–bullet', and that this is the only night of the year that they can be obtained. Intrigued, and unaware of the price he will have to pay, Max agrees to go with Kaspar to the Wolf's Glen at midnight. After Max leaves, Kaspar rejoices that he has found his substitute soul (*Schweig' – damit dich Niemand warnt! – Keep silent that none may warn you*).

Act 2. begins in the front room of Kuno's hunting lodge. Ännchen, Agathe's cousin, is standing on a ladder to rehang a portrait of the original Kuno, which had fallen down and struck Agathe on the head. In a delightful duet (*Schelm, halt' fest – Rogue, hold fast*) the girls sing lightly about the wickedness of the nail which permitted the picture to fall. Agathe comments that for Ännchen everything is a party, while she herself suffers with anxiety for Max. Ännchen, hoping to cheer her cousin, sings of her happy philosophy of love and flirting (*Kommt ein schlanker Bursch gegangen – When a slim young man comes along*). Agathe, who is putting ribbons on the white wedding dress she is making, joins in on the last line, but she remains pensive. Earlier that day she visited a hermit who gave her some white roses and warned her of a great danger; now the falling of the picture seems to her an evil omen. After Ännchen leaves, she opens the door to the balcony, and, seeing the beauty of the night, steps out. Her aria (*Leise, leise, fromme Weise – Softly, softly, my pure song*) becomes a prayer for protection from danger. Suddenly her mood changes to joy as Max approaches and enters with Ännchen to show

---

Samiel, the Black Huntsman, offers magic bullets to young men in exchange for their souls. (Covent Garden, 1961)

Agathe the eagle's plumage and to tell her of his good luck. He notices that she has been hurt, and Ännchen tells him about the picture. It was really Agathe's fault that the picture fell, she says, because just after seven o'clock she kept running to the window looking for Max, although she really had no reason to expect him so early. Max muses that it must have happened at the same time that he shot the eagle. Nevertheless he tells the girls that he must leave at once, and to conceal his true purpose he says that he has shot a huge stag near the infamous Wolf's Glen and must go back to get it. A trio follows (*Wie? Was? Entsetzen! – What? Where? Horror!*) in which Ännchen and Agathe voice their fear for Max, and Max resolutely bids them farewell.

Scene 2. takes place in moonlight in the Wolf's Glen, a lonely spot in the mountains near a waterfall. Invisible spirits chant a monotone song as Kaspar lays out a circle of stones around a skull. Nearby are the eagle's wings and a bullet mould. Kaspar plunges his hunting knife into the skull, raises it in the air and turning around three times calls on Samiel to appear. The Black Huntsman arrives, and Kaspar, whose term of life is almost up, begs for mercy. He has brought Samiel a substitute sacrifice, a young man in search of magic bullets. Samiel has only to direct the seventh bullet toward Agathe to bring Max to a despair that will make him the Devil's own. Samiel grants another three years of life to Kaspar, but warns him that he must have Max's soul or Kaspar's without fail on the morrow. He then vanishes, and suddenly the skull and hunting knife are replaced by a small fire. As Kaspar prepares to mould the bullets, Max appears on the cliff above and begins to climb down into the glen. The ghost of his dead mother rises from her grave in warning and he sees a vision of Agathe throwing herself into the waterfall, but his determination carries him on. Together he and Kaspar mould the bullets. After the sixth bullet is cast, cries of an invisible chorus are heard, the sky turns black and a huge storm arises. As Kaspar calls 'seven', Max takes the fatal step inside the circle of stones, repeating after Kaspar Samiel's name. Buffeted by the wind, he is blown out of the circle and clings to a rotten tree. Suddenly the storm ceases and Max finds that he is grasping the hand of the Black Huntsman. At the sign of the cross, Samiel vanishes.

Act 3. usually begins in Agathe's room, where she is trying on her wedding dress. She sings of her faith in God's love, even if this should be her last day on earth (*Und ob die Wolke sie verhülle – Even when the clouds hide it*). Ännchen enters, chiding her cousin for her mournful thoughts. Agathe relates that during the night she dreamed that she had been transformed into a white dove and that Max had unwittingly shot her. In an attempt to be comforting, Ännchen tells how a cousin of hers once dreamed of a monster which turned out to be only the watchdog (*Einst träumte meiner sel'gen Base – Once my late cousin dreamed*). Seeing that

Agathe is still unhappy, she tells her that such a sad expression does not befit a bride (*Trübe Augen – Sad eyes*). As she leaves the room, the bridesmaids enter dancing and singing a folk-like song (*Wir winden dir den Jungfernkranz – We're twining for you a maiden's wreath*). Ännchen returns with a box for Agathe, remarking that the portrait has fallen down again. Agathe opens the box, expecting to find her bridal wreath, but the box contains instead a funeral wreath. At this Ännchen takes the white roses, gift of the hermit, and twines them into a wreath for Agathe.

The final scene takes place in the forest where Prince Ottokar is making merry with his men before the trial shot. Kaspar is watching the proceedings from behind a tree. Although the trial shot was to have taken place before Agathe's arrival, she enters just as Max raises his gun to shoot a white dove pointed out to him by Ottokar. Agathe calls to Max, begging him not to shoot as she herself is the dove; but he fires the fatal seventh bullet, and both Agathe and Kaspar fall to the ground. Shocked, the chorus sings that Max has shot his own bride (*Schaut, O schaut! – Look, oh look!*). However Agathe is not dead. She has only fainted; it was Kaspar who was shot. Gasping for breath, Kaspar reveals that, at the crucial moment, the hermit stood beside Agathe and protected her. Alone of all the crowd able to see Samiel, he curses him and dies. Shocked, Ottokar orders his body to be thrown into the Wolf's Glen and demands the truth from Max, who confesses all (*Herr, unwerth bin ich Eurer Gnade – Sir, I am unworthy of your mercy*). In anger Ottokar orders him to be banished and forbids his marriage to Agathe. Suddenly the hermit reappears to suggest that Max's error does not deserve so great a punishment, and Ottokar at once agrees to support whatever decision the holy man may reach. The hermit suggests that the trial shot be abolished and that Max be put on a year's probation, at the end of which, if his behaviour has been satisfactory, he may marry Agathe (*Leicht kann des Frommen Herz auch wanken – Even the pious heart can wander*). The Prince supports the hermit's judgement, and as the opera ends all praise God, in whose gentleness all may trust.

French Grand Opera – Giacomo Meyerbeer

At the beginning of the 19th century, French and Italian opera developed certain individual characteristic features of style. While the French *grand opéra* and the Italian *melodramma* occasionally borrowed from each other's traditions, and while many 19th-century composers wrote operas in both styles, the two types of opera remained clearly distinct and separate.

French *grand opéra* had grown up independently from *opéra comique*, which continued to employ spoken dialogue and music of a popular nature. *Grand opéra* followed the traditions established by Jean-Baptiste Lully and his talented successor, Jean Philippe Rameau (1683–1764). Spectacle, not to say circus theatre, plays an important role in this form, which employs numerous sets and scene changes. Most grand operas run five acts, and performance time is considerable. An important feature is the inclusion of at least one ballet, usually a long one. The chorus also plays an important role, and it often functions as an independent dramatic force. Plots tend to deal with the recreation of a certain period or historical event in great detail, though not necessarily with great accuracy, and the emphasis is placed on the significance of these events themselves and not on the development of the individual characters. Recitative is the vehicle used for carrying forward the dramatic action and explaining the events of the plot; arias continue to be relatively static from a dramatic point of view. Libretti dealing with superstition, romance and horror predominate. *Grand opéra* presents many opportunities for vocal brilliance, though it does not pander to singers to the extent that the Italian *melodramma* does.

The French *grand opéra* was incarnate in the works of Giacomo Meyerbeer (1791–1864), who was born in Berlin but made his career in Paris. Building on the foundation laid by Spontini and by Daniel François Esprit Auber (1782–1871), Meyerbeer brought the form to perfection. His compositions dominated the operatic world during the 1830s and 1840s, and his influence can be seen in numerous composers who wrote in the second half of the 19th century. It was only at the very end of the century that French *grand opéra* began to fade in importance.

The style of Meyerbeer's music is not one that readily commends itself to modern audiences, although it was much admired by the public throughout the 19th century. His scores are long and elaborate, containing many scenes; vocal fireworks are included without apparent dramatic justification; and his melodic style strikes the ear as obvious and slightly crude. To appreciate his operas, it is necessary to realize that Meyerbeer was writing for a public that demanded exactly these qualities.

Meyerbeer's first opera, *Robert le Diable* (*Robert the Devil*) was premièred at the Paris Opéra on November 21, 1831, and won an immediate and tremendous success. It includes enormous crowd scenes, a church scene with an on-stage organ, and a ballet in which the spirits of defrocked nuns rise from their graves. The librettist of this work, Augustin Eugène Scribe (1791–1861), who was to become one of the best known librettists of *grand opéra*, was much influenced in his treatment of the magical and demonic elements of the libretto by Weber's *Der Freischütz*, which had been performed in Paris in 1824 as *Robin des bois*. The character Scribe created in Alice, a sweet and innocent young peasant girl, is one that dominates French libretti throughout the 19th century.

If *Robert le Diable* was a great success, it was overshadowed by the acclaim given to *Les Huguenots*, which was premièred in 1836, also at the Opéra. This work, also written to a libretto by Scribe, exemplifies many of the conventions of *grand opéra*: a historical subject; elaborate and varied scene changes and five acts; the obligatory ballet; and an omnipresent chorus.

Les Huguenots is set against the historical conflict of the Catholics and the Huguenots (French Protestants) in 16th-century France and deals with the events that led up to the St Bartholomew's Day Massacre on August 25, 1572. The prelude is based on the famous Reformation hymn by Martin Luther, *'Ein' feste Burg'* (*A mighty fortress*), and leads directly into the first act. This begins in a banquet hall in the castle of the Count de Nevers, a prominent Catholic, who welcomes to his party a young Huguenot nobleman, Raoul de Nangis. Nevers, who is to be married the following day, remarks to Raoul that he seems withdrawn, and suggests that perhaps he too is in love. Raoul confesses that he loves a lady whose name he does not know. He only saw her once, when he rescued her from an attack by some students.

A servant reports that a beautiful lady has arrived and has asked to speak with the Count in the garden. Nevers leaves at once to see her, as his guests speculate on what is happening, finally going to the windows to spy on the couple. Raoul recognizes his love, the lady from the carriage. Disgusted at finding her in this tête-à-tête with Nevers, his love turns to hate and he leaves the room. Nevers returns to announce that the lady was his fiancée, Valentine, who has come to break off their engagement by order of Queen Marguerite, to whom she acts as lady-in-waiting. Then a page brings a royal letter to Raoul, who has now returned, commanding him to permit himself to be blindfolded and taken by carriage to visit the writer of the letter, obviously the Queen. As the company congratulates him, several masked men blindfold him and lead him away.

Act 2. begins in the garden of Queen Marguerite's castle. Valentine tells the Queen that she has broken off her engagement to Nevers, and Marguerite explains that she has arranged a new engagement for her, to Raoul de Nangis, who is coming to see her today. Raoul arrives, and the Queen tells him that she has decided to arrange a marriage between him and Valentine, the daughter of the Catholic Count de St Bris, to strengthen the uneasy peace between Catholics and Protestants. St Bris, Nevers and members of the court arrive, and Marguerite announces the engagement, but when Valentine is presented to Raoul, he at once recognizes her as the lady in the garden and refuses to marry her. St Bris

and Nevers, offended, swear revenge. Marguerite does her best to prevent hostilities, but the act ends in confusion.

Act 3. takes place on the banks of the River Seine in Paris near several taverns and a church. A Catholic procession, followed by St Bris, Nevers and Valentine, moves towards the church where Valentine is to marry Nevers. Marcel, Raoul's servant, enters, demanding to speak with St Bris. The townspeople tell him to show more respect, and in anger he declares that his respect belongs to God alone. The incipient fight is interrupted by a group of gypsies who arrive selling their wares and dancing. [Some excuse for a ballet must be found.] Nevers, St Bris and Maurevert, a Catholic nobleman, leave the church without Valentine, who has stayed to pray. Marcel hands St Bris a letter from Raoul challenging him to a duel. St Bris accepts the challenge but forbids Maurevert, who has overheard, to mention it to Nevers, for he does not wish to risk the life of his son-in-law. Maurevert has another solution, however, and returning to the church, the two men plan an ambush. Valentine, overhearing the plot, realizes that she must save Raoul, whom she loves, and preserve her father's honour. She warns Marcel, but unfortunately Raoul has already left to fight the duel. Raoul and St Bris enter with their seconds, Raoul disregarding Marcel's warning. To cause a diversion, Marcel charges at Maurevert accompanied by two armed men, claiming that the Catholics are intruders. They exchange insults and are joined by Huguenot soldiers and a group of Catholic students. As fighting begins, Queen Marguerite arrives and chides them for failing to keep their oaths. Marcel tells her of the plot against Raoul and points out Valentine as his informer. St Bris is shocked by his daughter's behaviour, and Raoul is struck by her concern for him. St Bris is adamant, however, that Valentine shall marry Nevers, and the two leave on the nuptial barge while Raoul is comforted by Marcel.

Act 4. takes place on St Bartholomew's Day in an apartment in Nevers' castle in Paris. As Valentine grieves over her loss of Raoul, he suddenly enters, telling her that he must see her once again before he dies. He hides as Nevers and St Bris arrive with news of a plot to massacre the Huguenots: at the sound of the bells which will ring to celebrate the wedding of Queen Marguerite and Henry of Navarre (a Huguenot prince), Catholic forces will attack the Huguenots who are present in the city for the festivities. The conspirators leave to carry out their plans. Valentine and Raoul are unable to decide what to do, and as they hesitate,

In this 19th-century illustration Valentine tries to restrain Raoul from leaving through the window as the St Bartholomew's Day Massacre begins.

the bells begin to toll. They look down on the massacre beginning in the street below, and Valentine faints as Raoul leaves by the window.

As act 4. opens, a ball attended by a large number of Huguenot nobility is taking place to celebrate the marriage of Marguerite and Henry. A ballet is in progress when Raoul, covered with blood, arrives to warn them of the massacre. The men leave, drawing their swords and swearing revenge.

Scene 2. takes place in the cloister of a Huguenot church. Valentine, Raoul and Marcel, who is wounded, appear. Valentine counsels Raoul to renounce his faith and to appeal to the Queen for protection, but he refuses. Finally, out of love for him, she renounces her Catholicism and Marcel blesses her marriage to Raoul. As they join the other Huguenots in singing the hymn 'Ein' feste Burg', Catholic soldiers burst in, calling on them to recant. They refuse and are dragged away.

Scene 3. takes place in a Paris street. Marcel and Valentine are supporting Raoul, who has been mortally wounded in their escape from their captors. St Bris appears at the head of a group of soldiers and demands the identity of the threesome, whereupon Raoul answers that they are Huguenots. St Bris immediately orders the soldiers to open fire, realizing only afterwards that he has ordered the death of his own daughter. Queen Marguerite's carriage appears, returning from the ball. In vain she tries to quiet the shouts of the soldiers as the curtain falls.

Meyerbeer wrote four more operas after *Les Huguenots*, of which *Le Prophète* (*The Prophet* – 1849) and *L'Africaine* (*The African Girl*– premièred posthumously in 1865) were the most popular.

Two other French composers of the period deserve mention. Jacques Fromental Halévy (1799–1862) is particularly known for his opera *La Juive* (*The Jewess* – 1835) and was also the teacher of both Gounod and Bizet. Hector Berlioz (1803–69) is more often remembered for his symphonic music. Working in the shadow of Meyerbeer, he always had difficulty in getting his works performed. Among them are *Benvenuto Cellini* (1838), *Les Troyens* (*The Trojans* – performed complete only in 1890), and *La Damnation de Faust* (*The Damnation of Faust* – performed only in 1893). Like Halévy, he was a teacher of Gounod.

The Italian Melodramma – Donizetti and Bellini

The Italian *melodramma* (literally, 'music drama') was foreshadowed in the operas of Rossini and was further developed by Donizetti and Bellini. Italian opera of this period was often performed in small local theatres without extensive resources for production, and as a result there was little emphasis placed on elaborate scene changes or spectacles. It also meant that most works were performed by a resident company and had to be tailored to a typical staff. There are usually three main characters – a soprano, a tenor and a baritone. A second line of characters included another soprano or mezzo-soprano who played the part of confidante to the *prima donna* (first woman soloist), and a servant or messenger, which might be sung by any voice type. A *melodramma* was usually composed in two or three acts, rather than the five of a *grand opéra*. Ballets were rare.

In order to be successful, directors of Italian theatres had to avoid conflict with the omnipresent censors, whether of the church or of the state. This limited the choice of subject matter and reinforced a tendency to concentrate on the individual emotions of the very human characters while ignoring any abstract historical or social implications. The scarcity of spoken theatre during the first half of the 19th century was also partly attributable to censorship, and aside from a few remnants of the earlier street theatre, the *commedia dell'arte*, opera had no competition for an audience. Nonetheless, the theatre managers did have to 'sell' their entertainment, and they were not unaware that an elaborate display of vocal expertise by a favourite singer would always bring the house down. As a result, despite a continuing attempt by composers to control additions to or elaborations of their scores, the singers usually had the upper hand. When the *prima donna* appeared after the opening chorus, she expected to have her own *scena* (scene), composed according to the pattern set by Rossini. Near the end of the opera she expected to have a *gran' scena* (great scene), where she could display both her dramatic and vocal powers to her own – and the audience's – satisfaction. The bulk of the plot is not carried by recitative, as in the *grand opéra*, but rather in arias and ensembles. Climaxes intended to provoke applause were built into the ends of acts and scenes.

An important innovation of *melodramma* was the 'sad ending'. The theme is usually love, but love in the context of the other passions it arouses: jealousy, hatred and revenge. Plots concentrate on the tragedies caused by these emotions. Originality was not required of a 19th-century Italian librettist. Instead, he was expected to provide many reworkings of the same love story in new shadings of colour.

Gaetano Donizetti (1797–1848) began his career as an imitator of Rossini, but soon he found his own niche and composed sixty-four operas. His music is filled with catchy, easily remembered melodies, which were one of the main factors in his popularity. His rhythm swings, and he achieved syncopated (off-beat) accents by the use of a *sforzando* (a sudden loud/soft). He affords singers every possible opportunity to display their voices and vocal techniques, particularly in the *cadenza* (an inserted musical passage full of runs and trills) at the end of the *cavatina* and in the elaborate coloratura writing in the following *cabaletta*. The

Adelina Patti (1843–1919) as Lucia. Born in Madrid, Patti came to
the U.S. as a child and made her first public appearance at the age
of seven. She is considered to be one of the most celebrated
coloratura sopranos of all time.

chorus is used extensively, not for dramatic purposes, but to support the
solo voices, and the orchestra, offering little independent interest, serves
the same function. The declamation of important lines in parallel octaves
(a feature originated by Spontini) is used to great effect in his operas.

His comic operas, the ultimate echo of the 18th-century *opera buffa*, are
usually considered to be his best works. Among them are *L'elisir
d'amore* (*The Elixir of Love* – 1832), *La Fille du Régiment* (*The Daughter of
the Regiment* – 1840) and *Don Pasquale* (1843). However, Donizetti is
unquestionably best remembered for his tragedy, *Lucia di Lammermoor*,
which was premièred at the Teatro San Carlo in Naples on September
26, 1835.

Lucia was an immediate success. The libretto, written by Salvatore
Cammarano (1801–1852), is based on *The Bride of Lammermoor* by Sir
Walter Scott (1771–1832), the inventor of the historical novel. This
tragic story had its roots in real life: a forced separation of lovers and the
arranged marriage of the young woman to another man.

The opera is set against the background of a longstanding feud between the families of Lammermoor and Ravenswood. Enrico, head of the Lammermoor family, has seized the estates of Edgardo of Ravenswood but is now himself threatened by the King for his unfortunate political associations. To safeguard himself he is plotting to marry his sister Lucia to Arturo Bucklaw, an influential and wealthy noble.

The characteristically short prelude, containing strong musical contrasts, hints at the tragedy to follow. It leads immediately into Act 1. which begins in the grounds of Ravenswood Castle. Normanno, Enrico's Captain of the Guard, is searching for a stranger who has been seen in the area. Enrico confesses to Normanno and Raimondo, Lucia's tutor, that he fears that Edgardo has been meeting Lucia in secret. In a rage (*Cruda, funesta smania* – *A cruel, deathly fury*), he vows to prevent a union between the lovers.

Scene 2. takes place near a ruined fountain, where Lucia and Alisa, her companion, await Edgardo's coming. In a *cavatina* Lucia relates to Alisa the story of a maiden who was killed by her lover and thrown into that very fountain (*Regnava nel silenzio* – *Silence reigned*). When Alisa urges her to give up her dangerous secret meetings with Edgardo, she refuses and in the *caballeta* sings instead of her joy in his love (*Quando, rapita in estasi* – *When rapt in extasy*). As Alisa keeps watch, Edgardo arrives to bid Lucia farewell, for he finds he must leave for France. Confessing his previous intention of vengeance against her entire family for the murder of his father by Enrico, he tells her that her love has changed him (*Sulla tomba che rinserra* – *On the tomb which encloses*), although he still feels that he must seek revenge for his father's death. Exchanging vows and rings, they bid each other farewell (*Verrano a te sull'aure* – *Born to you on the breeze*).

Act 2. begins in Enrico's apartment in Ravenswood Castle. Normanno and Enrico plot to turn Lucia against Edgardo, who has been in France for some time. As Lucia enters, singing that Enrico's harshness has made her miserable (*Il pallor funesto* – *The deadly pallor*), Enrico continues to press his suggestion that she marry Arturo. To help achieve his goal he hands her a forged letter which makes it clear that Edgardo now loves another. In the following duet (*Soffriva nel pianto* – *I suffered in tears*), she laments her betrayal, while Enrico tries to convince her of her folly. They are interrupted by the sound of cheering and joyful music. Enrico reports that Arturo has arrived and that he and Lucia are to be wed at once. As he leaves, he warns Lucia that only her marriage can save him from political ruin and even death (*Se tradirmi tu potrai* – *If you betray me now*). Raimondo finally convinces her that marriage is the only way out (*Ah! cedi* – *Ah! yield*). Weeping, she agrees (*Guidami tu* – *Guide me*).

Scene 2. takes place in the great hall at Ravenswood Castle. The marriage deeds, ready for signing, lie on a table. A crowd of wedding guests rejoices (*Per te d'immenso giubilo – For you with great joy*) as Arturo expresses his friendship for Enrico (*Per poco fra le tenebre – For a while in the shadow*). Accompanied by Alisa, Lucia enters, pale and distraught. No sooner has she signed the marriage contract than Edgardo arrives. In the famous sextet that follows (*Chi mi frena in tal momento? – What holds me back at this moment?*), Edgardo meditates on avenging his father's death, Enrico is suddenly struck with remorse, Lucia wishes for death, and Raimondo, Arturo and Alisa comment on the tragic course that events have taken. Only now is Edgardo made aware that Lucia has actually married Arturo, and his love for her turns to rage. He angrily returns her ring and demands that she return his.

Act 3. usually begins with the famous 'mad scene'. Wedding celebrations are in progress in the great hall at Ravenswood (*D'immenso giubilo – Of great rejoicing*), when Raimondo enters to tell a grisly tale (*Dalle stanze ove Lucia – In the apartments where Lucia*). Hearing screams from the bridal chamber, he entered it to find that Lucia had stabbed Arturo with his

Joan Sutherland as the mad, bloodstained Lucia. (Covent Garden, 1959)

own dagger and is now completely insane. The guests are shocked still more when Lucia herself enters, dishevelled and pale. In the elaborate coloratura singing which follows, Lucia expresses her belief that she is with Edgardo and preparing for her wedding. Enrico enters and is stunned by her condition, but Lucia herself remains oblivious of him and continues to sing of her beloved, whom she begs to weep for her on earth as she will pray for him in heaven (*Spargi d'amaro pianto – Scatter bitter tears*). Struck with remorse, Enrico turns on Normanno and, accusing him of being an informer, orders him banished.

The final scene takes place near the tombs of the Ravenswoods at night. Edgardo earlier had been challenged to a duel by Enrico, and now, as he awaits him, he muses on Lucia's treachery and foretells his own death (*Fra poco a me ricovero – Before long I will be sheltered*). People of Lammermoor enter, lamenting Lucia's madness and impending death. As they tell Edgardo of the events at the castle, the death knell begins to toll. Raimondo comes to console Edgardo, but in vain. Instead Edgardo promises to join Lucia in death (*Tu che a Dio spiegasti l'ali – You who have taken wing to God*) and stabs himself. As the people pray for him, he dies in the hope of being reunited with Lucia in Heaven.

Vincenzo Bellini (1801–1835) was primarily a composer of tragic operas. His total output is not large (eleven operas), for he died at the age of thirty-four. His lyric melodic genius and sure dramatic sense led him to be admired not only by the public but also by other composers – even Wagner admired Bellini. In his music as in Donizetti's only one melody of importance occurs at a time, but that melody is given a reasonably interesting harmonic and instrumental treatment. He utilized the same forms for scenes and arias as did Donizetti, but is distinguished by a gentler and less bombastic style, with fewer of Donizetti's sudden contrasts. He was especially concerned about the texts that he set and worked closely with his librettists.

After three early operas, Bellini established his reputation with *La Sonnambula* (*The Sleepwalker* – 1831). Later that same year, on December 26, *Norma* was premièred at the Teatro alla Scala in Milan. Many consider this to be Bellini's finest opera.

Norma is related by subject to *grand opéra*, but the emphasis on the human element of the story instead of on the clash between the Druids and the Romans places it in the category of the *melodramma*. The talented librettist Felice Romani (1788–1865) wrote the libretto in consultation with Bellini, deriving much of his material from a play by Alexandre Soumet. The libretto is unusual in its emphasis on compassion and renunciation: Norma spares the lives of her children and gives her own life for her lover.

At the time of the story, around 50 B.C., Gaul was under the control of

Joan Sutherland (Australian soprano, b. 1926) as Norma,
surrounded by priests and priestesses before she cuts the sacred
mistletoe (Covent Garden, 1967). After her overnight success in
Lucia di Lammermoor in 1959, Sutherland began an international
career which has established her as one of the world's leading
sopranos.

Rome. The Druids were an ancient religious order who managed to
maintain their rites and some of their influence under the occupation.
The martial overture begins with a call to arms and then introduces the
theme of the Druid priests and Gallic warriors which will be heard again
in the first act.

Act 1. begins in the sacred grove of the Druids. The Druid priests and
the Gallic warriors enter to a march, followed by Oroveso, the high

priest and father of Norma, the high priestess. He urges the Druids to observe the rising of the new moon from the hill (*Ite sul colle – Go to the hill*), for when the moon has risen, Norma will come to the altar to prophesy. As the priests leave, they beg the gods to rouse their people against the Romans. Pollione, the Roman proconsul, enters with Flavio, his centurion. In remorse Pollione confesses that he no longer loves Norma, who broke her vow of chastity to become the mother of his two children. He now desires Adalgisa, a temple virgin, but is tormented by the thought of Norma's vengeance when she discovers his betrayal (*Meco all'altar di Venere – With me at the altar of Venus*). The Druids return, and as Pollione leaves with Flavio, he meditates on how to defeat their plots against him (*Traman congiure i barbari – The barbarians are conspiring against me*). Norma enters with her priestesses and is hailed by the Druid chorus. Oroveso asks how much longer they must submit to Rome, but in answer Norma warns that Rome will not fall at their hands. Counselling patience, she cuts the sacred mistletoe, singing her lyrical prayer to the moon, the famous aria '*Casta diva*' (*Chaste goddess*). After the Druids leave, Adalgisa remains alone in the grove to pray. She has broken her vow of chastity with her lover, Pollione, who now enters to find her. At first shunning his advances, she eventually is won over and agrees to meet him again in the grove on the following day.

Scene 2. takes place outside Norma's house. Norma bids farewell to her two children and tells Clotilde, her companion, that Pollione is being recalled to Rome and that she does not know if he plans to take her with him. Adalgisa timidly enters to reveal that she intends to leave her faith and land to go to Rome with her lover. Compassionately Norma releases her from her vows and tells her to go. Unfortunately Pollione enters at that moment, and Adalgisa reveals that he is her lover. The following trio expresses Norma's disgust at Pollione's behaviour, Adalgisa's anguish for Norma and Pollione's pleading on behalf of his new love. In the end Adalgisa refuses to go with him, and Norma swears that her betrayal shall be avenged.

Act 2. begins inside Norma's house. Norma enters with a dagger as her children sleep. She sings briefly of her love for them (*Teneri figli – Tender children*) as she steels herself to kill them, but she finds that she cannot do the deed and ends by throwing her arms around them and sobbing. She then sends for Adalgisa, whom she begs to take the children to Rome with their father. Adalgisa refuses, saying that instead she will go to plead Norma's case with Pollione. In duet (*Mira, O Norma – See, O Norma*), the two women pledge their friendship to each other.

Scene 2. takes place near the Temple of Irminsul. Norma enters, confident that Adalgisa will persuade Pollione to return to her, but Clotilde reports that Pollione was unmoved by Adalgisa's pleas. In anger

Norma strikes the shield to call an assembly. She announces that the time for war has come, and a fiery chorus follows (*Guerra! Guerra! – War! War!*). Oroveso demands from Norma the name of the victim for the ritual sacrifice, but she answers cryptically that a victim will be supplied when the time comes. Clotilde enters with the news that a Roman has been captured desecrating the virgins' cloister. As Gallic guards enter with Pollione, Norma raises her dagger to kill him but is unable to do so. She excuses herself, saying that she must first question him to find out if he had any accomplices. All leave them alone.

Pollione is now in Norma's power, and she urges him to return to her for the sake of his children (*In mia man alfin tu sei – You are at last in my hands*). Finding him unmoved, she tells him that she will appoint Adalgisa as the sacrifice as his punishment for his betrayal. She calls back the Druids and warriors and announces that the sacrificial victim will be a priestess who has broken her vows and has betrayed her gods and nation. As the funeral pyre is prepared, she begs her father to protect her children from the anger that is sure to rise against them and finally confesses that she herself is to be the victim. Pollione, brought to remorse at last, agrees to join in her sacrificial death.

Another opera by Bellini which remains in the contemporary repertory is *I Puritani* (*The Puritans* – 1835).

Italian Opera in the Last Half of the 19th Century – Verdi

Two names dominated the opera world during the last half of the 19th century – Verdi and Wagner. Verdi brought the tradition of the Italian *melodramma* to its highest point; Wagner created an elevated and intellectual opera based on mythology. Verdi is the successor of Mozart and Rossini; Wagner, the spiritual descendant of the composers of French *grand opéra* and of the German romantic opera of Weber.

Giuseppe Verdi (1813–1901) was born into a poor family in a small town, and it was only at considerable sacrifice that his family was able to pay for his music lessons. Verdi's early career was not inspiring: he failed to pass the examinations for admission to the Conservatory in Milan and his first operas were spectacularly unsuccessful. Only with the première of *Nabucco* (1842) did he achieve a measure of success. This opera, which tells the story of the Jews during the Babylonian captivity, strongly appealed to the Italians who at that time saw their country divided and under the domination of several foreign powers. Other operas with political overtones soon followed: *I Lombardi* (*The Lombards* – 1843), *Ernani* (1844), *I due Foscari* (*The Two Foscaris* – 1844), *Giovanna d'Arco* (*Joan of Arc* – 1845), *Attila* (1846), *La battaglia di Legnano* (*The Battle of*

84

Legnano – 1849). Verdi's name itself became a rallying cry for the unification of Italy under Victor Emanuel, King of Sardinia – *Vittorio Emanuele Re D'Italia* – and the cry '*Viva Verdi*' indicated far more than an enthusiasm for his music. Intensely patriotic, Verdi even served his country as a member of the Italian parliament for a short period after the unification of Italy under Garibaldi in 1860.

As an opera composer, Verdi was plagued by many of the same problems that faced his immediate predecessors, Donizetti and Bellini. Singers still made most of the major musical decisions, deciding what they would condescend to sing and in what form they intended to sing it, and Verdi fought to have his scores performed as he wrote them for the better part of his life. He was also faced with certain orchestral limitations. Almost the entire musical output of Italy during the 19th century was dedicated to opera, as there were very few opportunities for the performance of instrumental compositions. Therefore it is not surprising that Italian orchestration techniques remained inferior to those elsewhere in Europe. Adding to this the traditional Italian emphasis on the singing voice, it is hardly surprising to find that opera composers, including Verdi, did not assign a particularly exciting role to the orchestra. Verdi relies on the voice as his dramatic tool; the orchestra is used to support and reinforce vocal melody and to provide a showcase for the singers' voices.

Verdi borrowed many of his forms and techniques from his predecessors. He wrote scenes for soloists in the *scena* form developed by Rossini and borrowed the on-stage band from the same source. Like his Italian predecessors, he was uninterested in an overall tonal unity of the sort achieved by Mozart. His operas are composed of 'numbers', each designed to fit the voices or dramatic needs of singers. As a result there is no necessary correlation of key between the two parts of an aria which make up a *scena*. There is no question, however, that Verdi had an excellent understanding of the capabilities of the human voice, and this, plus his genius for composing delightful and memorable melodies, was a major factor in his success.

Verdi reveals his most individual style in his ensembles. He enjoyed writing voice parts to conflict with each other in phrasing and in style, giving the effect both of dialogue and of contrasting emotion. He reserved the sweetness of parallel thirds and sixths, so beloved of Rossini and Bellini, for duets of love or reconciliation. While he did use melodic motives to tie together certain important points of dramatic action or entrances of specific characters, he did not develop a comprehensive system of *leitmotiv* in the Wagnerian manner, in which short melodic fragments consistently symbolize abstract qualities like hope or love.

It is hardly an accident that he drew upon some of the world's greatest

dramatists – Victor Hugo, Schiller, Shakespeare – for his plots. With the exception of *Falstaff* (1893), his final operatic triumph, and *Un giorno di regno* (*King for a Day* – 1840), an early failure in the *buffa* style, Verdi wrote no comic operas. Rather, his works tend to be serious, somewhat violent, and to end in tragedy.

Verdi's full power for dramatic expression, anticipated in *Macbeth* (1847) and *Luisa Miller* (1849), can be seen in *Rigoletto*, which was first performed at the Teatro La Fenice in Venice on March 11, 1851. The libretto is based on a play by Victor Hugo entitled *Le Roi s'amuse* (*The King is entertained*). Trouble with the censors might have been foreseen, as Hugo's play had been suspended from performance after the première in 1832. In response to their numerous demands the title was changed, the King (Francis I) became the Duke, and the 16th-century court of France was moved to the Duchy of Mantua. To make the necessary alterations, Verdi and his librettist, Francesco Maria Piave, were forced to postpone the opening performance for several months. When finally produced, *Rigoletto* was a tremendous success.

The brief prelude, which contains the music of the curse uttered by Count Monterone against Rigoletto, leads directly into the ballroom scene of Act 1. The act begins in a magnificent hall in the palace of the Duke of Mantua. The Duke reveals to Brosa, a courtier, that he is on the verge of succeeding in his conquest of a young girl whom he has been seeing at church for over three weeks. He has learned where she lives and has noted that every night a mysterious man goes there to see her. Expressing his careless philosophy of love in a lilting aria (*Questa o quella* – *This lady or another*), he begins to flirt with the attractive Countess Ceprano. Rigoletto, the hunchbacked court jester, enters and makes fun of her jealous husband. He even goes so far as to suggest to the Duke that he carry off the Countess as a joke. The Count is angered, and in the following ensemble (*Vendetta del pazzo!* – *Vengeance on the fool!*) he expresses his rage while the Duke defends Rigoletto. The courtiers break in, agreeing that Rigoletto has gone too far but suggesting that all relax and enjoy the party (*Tutto è gioia* – *All is joy*). Their gaiety is soon interrupted. Count Monterone arrives and angrily tries to call the Duke to account for seducing his daughter. Rigoletto seizes this opportunity to mock him. As the Duke orders the Count's arrest, Monterone turns on Rigoletto and curses him (. . . *tu che d'un padre ridi al dolore, sii maledetto* – *you who laugh at a father's grief, be accursed*) and also the Duke. As the courtiers demand that Monterone be led away, he repeats the curse, to Rigoletto's horror.

Tito Gobbi (Italian baritone, b. 1915) as the court jester Rigoletto in a 1966 BBC television programme.

Scene 2. takes place in front of Rigoletto's house at night. The jester enters, wrapped in a cloak, to meditate on the curse (*Quel vecchio maledivami – How the old man cursed me*). Sparafucile, a professional assassin, slyly suggests that he is available should Rigoletto ever need his assistance. The two sing a duet in which Sparafucile reveals how his pretty sister lures his victims to a rundown tavern where he dispatches them quickly and quietly. When Sparafucile leaves, Rigoletto ponders their similarities: he kills with his tongue, Sparafucile with his dagger (*Pari siamo! – We are alike*). Nature's gift to him of a deformed body has caused mankind to require that his mind become vicious as well. Pushing away his depressing thoughts, he opens the gate to meet his lovely daughter, Gilda, whom he permits to leave the house only to attend church. As usual Rigoletto is worried that Gilda might be abducted, and he orders Giovanna, Gilda's nurse, to guard his daughter closely. Footsteps are heard outside. As Rigoletto goes into the street to see who is there, the Duke slips inside the gate and hides. Not seeing anyone, Rigoletto returns to bid the ladies goodnight.

After he leaves, Gilda confesses to Giovanna that she did not tell her father about a young man who has been following her to church. As she sings about her admirer, the Duke breaks in to complete her sentence, signalling to Giovanna to leave. In duet the two sing of their love, and when Gilda asks his name, the Duke tells her that he is a poor student by the name of Gualtier (Walter) Maldè. Giovanna returns to warn the lovers that someone is coming, and the Duke departs. Alone, Gilda meditates on his beloved name (*Caro nome*) in one of Verdi's most beautiful arias, whose spirit of innocence and trust suggests her complete ignorance of the Duke's true name and character; and as she ascends the stairs to retire, she continues to repeat his name.

In the street a group of masked courtiers led by Count Ceprano meet Rigoletto. Marullo cunningly tells him that they are taking his advice to carry off the Countess Ceprano as a joke. Rigoletto joins them, asking for a mask. Marullo helps him to put one on, which effectively blindfolds him. They then ask him to hold the ladder, which he does. As they break not into Count Ceprano's house but into Rigoletto's, they sing how they will laugh at him tomorrow (*Zitti, zitti – Hush, hush*). As Rigoletto waits below, they carry off Gilda, who calls for help. Too late he realizes that he has fallen victim to a plot, and in anguish he recalls the curse (*La maledizione!*).

Act 2. takes place in a room in the Duke's palace. The Duke sings of how he went to visit Gilda only to find the house deserted (*Parmi veder le lagrime – I seem to see her tears*). The courtiers enter with news: they have carried off a woman whom they believe to be Rigoletto's mistress (*Scorrendo uniti remota via – We went together to a deserted street*). When he

Amelita Galli-Curci (Italian soprano, 1882–1963) who made her
Rome début as Gilda in *Rigoletto*. Mainly self-taught, she had
great charm and beauty of tone as a singer, though some critics
felt her technique lacked finish.

learns that she is in the palace, the Duke goes at once to see her. Rigoletto
arrives, pretending indifference, but actually looking around to see if
there is any evidence of Gilda's presence. Suddenly realizing that she is
with the Duke, he admits to the courtiers that she is his daughter and tries
to break into the Duke's room. Forcibly restrained, he is reduced to
begging them for mercy (*Cortigiani, vil razza dannata – Courtiers, you vile,
damned race*). Suddenly Gilda comes out and throws herself into her
father's arms, begging to speak to him alone. She then tells him the story
of her meetings with the Duke and their tragic result (*Tutte le feste al
tempio – All the feastdays at church*). As father and daughter mingle their
tears, Monterone passes through the room on his way to the dungeon.
Pausing before the Duke's portrait, he comments that his curse does not
seem to have taken effect. Rigoletto turns on the portrait, promising his
own revenge.

Act 3. takes place in front of a rundown inn near the river. Sparafucile
is inside, while Rigoletto and Gilda wait in the road to identify the Duke,
whom Gilda still loves. He enters the inn singing a drinking song whose

infectious melody has made it one of Verdi's best known arias (*La donna è mobile – Woman is fickle*). [Correctly anticipating the aria's popular appeal, Verdi withheld the music for it from his cast until the last minute, to prevent any 'leak' to the public before the première performance.] Maddalena, Sparafucile's sister, finds the Duke attractive and begins to flirt with him. When Sparafucile asks for confirmation of the Duke's identity, Rigoletto is evasive and promises to return later. In the following quartet – a masterpiece of ensemble writing – the Duke flirts with Maddalena while Gilda, in a soaring *obbligato*, laments her lover's unfaithfulness and Rigoletto darkly vows revenge (*Un di, se ben rammento mi – One day, if I recall correctly*). After Gilda leaves, Rigoletto makes the final arrangements with Sparafucile, saying that he will return at midnight to throw the body into the river. As he leaves, the Duke retires to sleep. A storm has come up, and Gilda comes back to the inn dressed in men's clothing. Listening at the window, she hears Sparafucile order Maddalena to mend a sack for the Duke's body. To please his sister, who rather likes the Duke and doesn't want him to be killed, Sparafucile agrees that if another traveller arrives before midnight he shall be killed in place of the Duke. To save her lover, Gilda knocks on the door and asks shelter for the night. She is immediately stabbed by Sparafucile.

Rigoletto returns for the body, pays the assassin and begins to drag the heavy sack towards the river. Suddenly the unmistakable voice of the Duke is heard singing his drinking song. Opening the sack, Rigoletto discovers his dying daughter who tells him, with her last breath, that she has sacrificed herself for the man she loves. Calling her name, Rigoletto remembers the curse (*Ah! La maledizione!*), and as the orchestra repeats the curse theme, the curtain falls.

The two operas which immediately follow *Rigoletto – Il trovatore* (*The Troubadour* – 1853) and *La traviata* (*The Courtesan* – also 1853) – are among Verdi's most performed works. *Il trovatore* is a violent, twisted tale in which a gypsy's vengeance brings two long-separated brothers to rivalry in love, mutual hatred and ultimately fratricide. Filled with strong, harsh music – the famous 'Anvil Chorus', for example, or the gypsy's '*Stride la vampa*' (*The blazing fire roared*) – it achieved immediate success. A different aspect of Verdi's genius is revealed in the initially unsuccessful *La traviata*, the touching story of a generous courtesan's love for a man of middle-class respectability. At the première performance the audience objected to its use of modern-day costumes, which perhaps brought the story too close to real life, and furthermore, a particularly fat soprano had been cast as the fragile heroine. When in the last act the doctor announced that she was dying of consumption (tuberculosis), the theatre was filled with roars of laughter. Soon, however, *La traviata*'s lyric beauty made it one of Verdi's most beloved operas.

Leontyne Price (b. 1927) as the slave girl, Aïda. An American
soprano, Price achieved her first success in *Porgy and Bess* and
went on to sing in San Francisco, Chicago, New York and many of
the great European opera houses.

After these two masterpieces came a series of successful works: *Les
Vêpres Siciliennes* (*The Sicilian Vespers* – 1855), a *grand opéra* for Paris;
Simon Boccanegra (1857); *Un ballo in maschera* (*A Masked Ball* – 1859),
whose plot, originally dealing with the assassination of King Gustav III
of Sweden, was shifted to 17th-century Massachusetts in order to satisfy

the censors; *La forza del destino* (*The Force of Destiny* – 1862), a *grand opéra* for St Petersburg; and *Don Carlos* (1867), another *grand opéra* for Paris. The influence of *grand opéra* is also evident in *Aïda* (1871). The grandeur of the French tradition is reflected in such aspects of the work as the triumphal march and the ballet, while the emphasis on romantic and human interests identify it as part of the Italian tradition of *melodramma*. It remains a 'numbers' opera, composed of many separate units, but the sections are more closely linked by thematic material and are written in a more unified style than was the case in any of Verdi's previous operas.

The composition of *Aïda* was originally requested by the Khedive of Egypt for the opening of the new Italian Opera House in Cairo. The Egyptian subject is based on a story by the French Egyptologist Auguste Mariette (the title 'Bey', which often follows his name, was given him by the Khedive for his scholarship). Verdi and Camille du Locle (1832–1903) developed a French scenario from the story, and then Antonio Ghislanzoni (1824–1893), a professional librettist with over fifty libretti to his credit, was asked to arrange the story in verse.

The opera was to have been presented in January of 1871, but in July of 1870 the Franco–Prussian war broke out, leaving Mariette, who was in charge of all the delicate negotiations with the Egyptians, stranded by the siege of Paris. The first performance was consequently postponed until December 24, 1871. Its resounding success was echoed by a performance six weeks later at La Scala in Milan.

The prelude presents both the theme of Aïda and of the priests, indicating the conflict of the opera to follow. Act 1. begins in the great hall of the Egyptian king's palace in Memphis. Radames, captain of the Egyptian guards, hopes to lead the Egyptian forces in their coming campaign against the Ethiopians. He dreams of returning to lay his victory at the feet of the little slave girl, Aïda, and in a famous tenor aria (*Celeste Aïda* – *Heavenly Aïda*) he sings of his love for this girl who rules his heart.

Amneris, daughter of the King, enters and suspiciously questions Radames, for she jealously suspects that he loves Aïda rather than her. When Aïda enters, pensive and withdrawn, Amneris questions her too, but she replies that she fears for the fate of her native land, Ethiopia. The King enters to announce that a messenger has arrived with grave tidings: the Ethiopians have invaded Egypt and are even now marching to Thebes under the leadership of King Amonasro himself. As the assembled Egyptians call for war, the King announces that the supreme commander named by Isis is Radames. Accompanied by the cheering crowd which cries '*Ritorna vincitor!*' (*Return victorious!*), he leaves for the Temple of Vulcan to don the sacred arms of the commander.

When everyone has left, Aïda repeats the phrase '*Ritorna vincitor*', as she begins an impassioned aria describing how she is torn between her love for Radames and her concern for her father. In anguish she prays to the gods for help and pity.

Scene 2. takes place in the Temple of Vulcan. A priestess chants the invocation to Phtha (the god of creation) and is answered by the priests. As the priestesses dance the sacred dance, Radames is led to the altar where Ramfis invests him with the sacred arms.

Act 2. begins in Amneris' apartment in the palace. Surrounded by slave girls, the Princess is dressing for the celebration of Radames' great victory. A group of Moorish slaves dance for her entertainment. As Aïda approaches, Amneris dismisses her attendants and speaks to her in pretended sympathy (*Fu la sorte dell' armi a' tuoi funesta* – *The fortunes of war have been tragic for you*). Resolved to trap Aïda into confessing her love for Radames, she reports that the commander was slain in battle. Aïda reveals her true feelings and begs for pity, telling Amneris that while the Princess has everything, she has only her love. As an off-stage chorus begins to sing the hymn of victory, Amneris leaves to play her role in the celebration, warning Aïda to remember that she is but a humble slave.

Scene 2. takes place at the entrance to the city of Thebes. A huge crowd has gathered to celebrate the triumph (*Gloria all' Egitto* – *Glory to Egypt*). Led by on-stage trumpeters, the 'Triumphal March' accompanies the army's entrance with its banners, chariots and images of the gods – and sometimes even live elephants! Dancing girls enter bearing the spoils of war. Finally Radames arrives, borne on a litter, to the cheers of the people Amneris places on his head the victor's crown, and the King promises that he will grant him any request. Radames orders that the prisoners be brought in, among whom is Amonasro, who warns Aïda not to identify him. Speaking for the captured Ethiopians, he reports that the King was killed in battle and asks mercy for the captives (*Ma tu, o re* – *But you, O King*). Radames then asks the King to redeem his pledge and to pardon the prisoners. The King agrees to this and also pledges to the hero the hand of his daughter Amneris, with whom he shall someday rule all of Egypt. Yet another triumphal chorus concludes the act.

Act 3. takes place on the banks of the Nile, near the Temple of Isis. Amneris, accompanied by a group of women and guards, is led by Ramfis into the temple to keep vigil on the eve of her wedding. Aïda enters, veiled, to wait for Radames, mourning that never again will she see her home (*O cieli azzurri* – *O azure heavens*). She is interrupted by her father, who persuades her to discover from Radames the battle plans against Ethiopia. He hides as Radames arrives. Aïda greets him with reserve, but when he swears that although he is now to wed Amneris he still loves only her, she relents. Nevertheless she urges him to flee with her to her native land (*Fuggiam gli ardori inospiti* – *Let us flee from the burning*

A scene from the 1979 English National Opera production of *Aïda*, with Josephine Barstow (far right) in the title role.

inhospitality). At first Radames refuses, but he eventually agrees with her (*Ah, no! Fuggiamo!* – *Ah, no! Let us flee*). When she asks how they are to avoid the Egyptians in their flight, he replies that it should be simple, as the armies do not plan to march through the Pass of Napata until the following day. Overhearing the army's route, Amonasro comes forward in excitement, promising that he and his forces plan to be there to meet them. Radames realizes in despair that he has betrayed his country, and Amneris, leaving the temple, calls out that he is a traitor. Telling Amonasro to flee with Aïda, he surrenders himself to the guards.

Act 4. begins in a large hall in the palace. Amneris orders the guards to bring Radames to her in one last attempt to save his life. Despite her advice and pleadings (*Già i sacerdoti adunansi* – *Now the priests are taking counsel together*), he remains resolved to die. When he has been returned to his cell, she gives voice to her despair (*Ohimè morir mi sento! – Alas, I shall die!*). The priests enter the underground judgement hall, and Radames is led through under guard. The charge against him is repeated three times, as Amneris, listening outside the chamber, prays to the gods for mercy. Then the sentence is announced by Ramfis: he must die the traitor's death and is to be entombed alive.

Scene 2. is played on two levels. The lower section of the stage reveals a dark tomb underneath the light-filled Temple of Vulcan. Radames is sitting on the steps that lead down into the tomb, reflecting that he will never again see the light of day or his beloved Aïda (*La fatal pietra – The fatal stone*). As he sings, a shadowy figure moves towards him. It is Aïda, who has come to share his death (*Presago il core della tua condanna – I sensed your condemnation in my heart*). As the chanting and ritual dances begin above them, they bid each other farewell (*O terra addio – O earth, farewell*). Amneris enters the upper temple to pray for Radames, and as Aïda dies in Radames' arms, the voice of the Princess is heard in prayer above the chanting of the priests (*Pace t'imploro – I pray for peace*).

Verdi wrote two operas after *Aïda*: *Otello* (1887), and *Falstaff* (1893). Both are based on plays by Shakespeare, with libretti by the opera composer and librettist Arrigo Boïto (1842–1918). These works, like most of Verdi's operas, continue to be regularly performed today.

The German Music Drama – Wagner

Just as Verdi dominated Italian opera during the last half of the 19th century, Richard Wagner (1813–1883) dominated German opera of the period. Born the same year as Verdi, Wagner's approach to opera composition was considerably different from that of his Italian contemporary. Verdi can be considered a successor to Rossini and the composers of early Italian *melodramma*, while Wagner is the successor of the composers of French *grand opéra* and of the early German Romantic operas of Weber.

The early works of Wagner (*Die Feen – The Fairies*, written *ca.* 1833; and *Das Liebesverbot – The Ban on Love*, written in 1835) reveal the influence of such diverse composers as Beethoven, Weber and Bellini. *Rienzi* (1842), a popular success, was constructed along the lines of a *grand opéra*, and *Der fliegende Holländer* (*The Flying Dutchman* – 1843), another popular opera, followed on demand. His next two operas, *Tannhäuser* (1845) and *Lohengrin* (1850), can be regarded as the transitional steps to his mature style. These two operas are at once the culmination of early 19th-century German romantic opera and the promise of the mythic works to come.

The Festspielhaus in Bayreuth, which was designed by Richard
Wagner specifically for the production of his music dramas.

Wagner himself wrote the libretti for his operas, intending to create a
unified work of art (*Gesamtkunstwerk*), complete in all details including
actual production. By the time he had completed *Lohengrin*, he had
arrived at a concept of art heavily influenced by contemporary German
philosophy, and he began to compose a series of mythological operas
dealing with abstract concepts such as love and death. The relationship of
ideas is far more important in these works than are the human relationships of the characters. Wagner's characters are intended to be abstract
and universal, and this is underscored by his choice of the gods as
protagonists in his operas. Events are simplified to reveal their inner
qualities, which are sustained by pure music.

Wagner eliminated the breaks between numbers or scenes, providing
orchestral interludes if necessary to create continuous action. He devoted
a great deal of consideration to the overall structure of his operas, which
are comprised of large musical forms. He developed to its full extent the
concept of *leitmotiv* to characterize certain concepts and ideas contained
in his works. A *leitmotiv* is a short musical fragment carried by the

orchestra (only rarely is one heard in the vocal line) which symbolizes an abstract idea or quality such as love. With this emphasis on the abstract, the role of the orchestra increased and the role of the human voice as a dramatic tool decreased. The vocal line is designed to declaim the text rather than to portray human emotion or gratify lovers of vocal fireworks. At the same time, Wagner placed heavy demands on his singers. The Wagnerian orchestra became much larger than the average opera orchestra of the day, particularly in the brass section and, to avoid drowning out the singers, it was arranged that the orchestra pit of Wagner's theatre at Bayreuth, Germany, should be covered. With the growth of the orchestra's role, Wagner became intensely interested in the development of harmony. He is credited with stretching the classical tonal system to its utmost limits and initiating the harmonic dissolution of the 20th century.

All of these features are evident in Wagner's cycle of four operas (tetralogy), which was meant to be played in a three-day sequence with an introductory evening before. This immense saga, *Der Ring des Nibelungen* (*The Ring of the Nibelungs*), was composed over a period of many years, from 1848 to 1874. In August of 1876, the first full performance took place at the Festspielhaus in Bayreuth, a theatre designed by Wagner and built with the assistance of his patron, King Ludwig II of Bavaria.

The first opera, *Das Rheingold* (*The Gold of the Rhine*), sets the scene and functions as a prelude to the three operas that follow. Scene 1. takes place in the bed of the Rhine River, where the Rhinemaidens are guarding the gold of the Rhine. According to tradition this gold can be forged into a ring which will make its owner the lord of the world. To forge the ring, however, one must renounce love forever. Alberich, an ugly dwarf, duly renounces love and steals the gold.

Scene 2. takes place at the castle of Valhalla where Wotan, the one-eyed ruler of the gods, and Fricka, his wife, have just awoken. Wotan has agreed to give Fricka's sister Freia, the goddess of youth and beauty, to the giants Fasolt and Fafner in exchange for building this castle for him. Freia now appears, seeking protection. The giants follow shortly, and Wotan tries to persuade them to accept another form of payment. Donner and Froh, Freia's brothers, arrive to protect her, and a fierce quarrel breaks out. At this point, Loge, the god of fire and Wotan's clever adviser, enters, announced by the magic fire *leitmotiv*. He reports that he has been unable to find another suitable reward for the giants, although he has searched the entire earth. He points out that only one man (Alberich) has ever voluntarily renounced love for another treasure. Intrigued by Loge's story, Fasolt and Fafner agree to accept the treasure instead of Freia, but Wotan refuses this arrangement. As a result the

A cut-away drawing (1885) of the trolleys used to let the
Rhinemaidens appear to be swimming on stage.

giants seize Freia and carry her off. Loge warns the other gods that since
the goddess of youth has been taken from them they now face old age
and mortality. Concerned about this, Wotan decides to search for
Alberich's treasure to ransom Freia.

Scene 3. takes place in Nibelheim, the underground home of the
Nibelungs, where Alberich is scolding Mime, his brother, for not finishing his forging work. As he is knocked around, Mime drops a helmet
called the *tarnhelm*, which has the power to make its wearer invisible.
Alberich puts it on and vanishes. Wotan and Loge arrive to discover that
Alberich has forged the magic ring, which has enabled him to discover an
enormous treasure in the ground that the Nibelungs are being forced to
mine for him. Alberich returns and suspiciously asks Wotan and Loge
their business. Wotan explains that they would like to see his treasure. To
trick Alberich, Loge asks him to display the power of the *tarnhelm* to
change the wearer into any shape he chooses. Boastful Alberich first
changes himself into a snake; then, taunted by Loge, into a toad. Wotan
immediately steps on the toad, while Loge seizes the *tarnhelm*. The gods
bind Alberich and take him away with them.

Scene 4. takes place in a rocky pass, where Wotan and Loge offer to
ransom Alberich in return for his treasure. Alberich reluctantly agrees,
and with the aid of his ring orders his slaves to bring it to them. The gods

demand the *tarnhelm* and finally also the ring. Alberich warns them that whoever steals the ring will be accursed, but Wotan, unintimidated, takes the ring. Reiterating the curse, Alberich vanishes. Wotan offers the treasure to the giants but tries to withhold the ring. Only when Erda, the earth goddess, appears to warn Wotan that the gods are doomed and that he must relinquish the ring, does he give it to the giants. They at once begin to fight over it, and Fasolt is killed. Fafner leaves with the treasure and his brother's body, and the gods return to Valhalla.

Die Walküre (The Valkyrie) is the second of the operas of the tetralogy. Suspecting that Alberich will make every effort to regain the ring from Fafner and use its power to destroy the gods, Wotan has ordered his nine daughters, the Valkyries, to bring to him the bodies of the world's bravest heroes. These he has transformed into immortals to protect the gods. Wotan has also tried to find a hero to recover the ring from Fafner, who is now guarding his treasure in the form of a dragon. He has hopes that Siegmund, a mortal son of his, will be able to do so.

Act 1. begins in a hut in the forest during a storm. Siegmund, fleeing from the attack of a group of foresters, seeks refuge. Sieglinde, wife of Hunding the forester, offers him water and mead as the love *leitmotiv* is heard in the orchestra. Having rested and regained some strength, Siegmund tries to leave but is detained by Sieglinde. Hunding enters, suspicious of his uninvited guest but extending nevertheless the traditional offer of hospitality. In conversation, Siegmund reveals that he returned home one day when he was a child to find his mother dead and his twin sister gone. Later he was also separated from his father, whom he did not know as Wotan but rather as Wälse, for which reason he calls himself Wälsung (*Son of Wälse*). He also reveals that he was just now involved in a fight with some foresters, and Hunding realizes that he has invited an enemy to be a guest in his home. Continuing to follow the rules of hospitality, he challenges him to a duel on the following day and retires with Sieglinde.

Sieglinde returns to Siegmund to tell her that during her wedding to Hunding a one-eyed stranger (Wotan) appeared and plunged a sword into a nearby ash tree, stating that it would belong to whoever could pull it out. Siegmund realizes that the stranger must have been his father, who once told him that he would be given a sword in his hour of need. He pulls out the sword, which he names '*Nothung*' ('*Needful*'), and its characteristic *leitmotiv* sounds in the orchestra. Sieglinde and Siegmund realize that they are brother and sister and joyously embrace.

Act 2. takes place on a mountain in the wilderness. Wotan orders his daughter Brünnhilde to lead the other Valkyries to the defense of Siegmund in his duel with Hunding. As she sings her war cry and leaves, Fricka enters, very angry. As the goddess of marriage, she cannot permit

Siegmund to steal Sieglinde from Hunding and forces Wotan to revoke his order to Brünnhilde. The Valkyrie comes upon the exhausted pair as they are fleeing from Hunding. She warns Siegmund of his coming death and promises that he will be taken to Valhalla. When he refuses to leave Sieglinde, however, Brünnhilde is won over and agrees to help him in defiance of her father's orders. Siegmund and Hunding meet, but Brünnhilde is defeated when Wotan appears to shatter Siegmund's sword, permitting Hunding to kill him. Gathering up the pieces of the broken sword, Brünnhilde flees with Sieglinde. At a gesture from Wotan, Hunding falls down dead.

Act 3. begins with the famous 'ride of the Valkyries', who are returning from battle to their mountaintop. Brünnhilde arrives with Sieglinde. The other Valkyries, fearing Wotan's wrath, are unwilling to help Sieglinde but suggest that she go to Fafner's cave, where she will surely be safe. Brünnhilde bids her farewell, prophesying that she will bear a son, Siegfried, who will be the greatest hero the world has ever known. Taking with her the pieces of the broken sword, Sieglinde leaves. Wotan approaches in a storm and orders the other Valkyries away. Brünnhilde is to be punished by being placed in a magic sleep until a man awakens her. Wotan makes only one concession to his daughter: while she sleeps, she will be protected by a wall of fire. He kisses her eyes, thereby taking away her godhood, and she falls asleep. Loge is ordered to surround her with fire, and the appropriate fire music is heard.

The third opera of the tetralogy is *Siegfried*. The son of Siegmund and Sieglinde, he has been brought up by Mime, who found Sieglinde after she left the Valkyries to search for Fafner's cave. Sieglinde died when Siegfried was born.

Act 1. begins in Mime's cave where he is forging yet another new sword for Siegfried, who breaks every sword he is given. Mime realizes that if he could only mend the broken sword 'Nothung', all his problems would be over, and perhaps Siegfried could even be induced to kill the dragon Fafner and recover the treasure. Siegfried arrives with a bear which chases Mime. Soon tiring of that sport, Siegfried picks up the sword which Mime has been working on and breaks it on the anvil, complaining that Mime can never seem to make a sword that is of any use to him. Suddenly he demands that Mime tell him about his parents. Mime relates the story of Sieglinde, telling Siegfried that she was the one who named him. All he knows of Siegfried's father is that he was killed in

---

Two contrasting conceptions for *Die Walküre*: (Above) a design by Joseph von Hoffman for his setting at the 1876 Bayreuth Festival; (Below) a stark, dramatic set for a 1964 Covent Garden performance.

The Nibelung dwarf, Mime. (Hans Breuer in a Bayreuth performance)

combat. When he shows Siegfried his father's broken sword, Siegfried demands that it be mended and leaves Mime in despair, because he knows he cannot do it. The Wanderer (Wotan in disguise) appears to challenge Mime to a contest. Each of them is to ask the other three questions and he who cannot answer is to forfeit his head. Mime's three questions, which recapitulate the action of the two previous operas, are easily answered by the Wanderer, who then asks his own questions. Mime is able to answer the first two, but the third question – the identity of the person who will mend the broken sword – he cannot answer. The Wanderer tells him that only one who is fearless can reforge the sword and departs. When Siegfried returns, Mime offers to take him to Fafner's cave so that he can try his luck. Seeing that the sword is not yet mended, Siegfried himself picks up the pieces and sets to work. Meanwhile Mime concocts a draught to poison Siegfried, so that should the hero actually kill the dragon, Mime will be able to steal the treasure for himself. Siegfried finishes the sword and splits the anvil in half with one blow.

Act 2. takes place in the woods near Fafner's cave. The Wanderer accosts Alberich, who is lurking in the shadows, and warns him that Mime is bringing the 'fearless boy' to kill Fafner, after which he plans to steal the ring for himself. Relieved that he is no longer contending with Wotan for the ring, Alberich agrees to go to wake Fafner and to offer him the chance of giving them the ring now in exchange for his life. The dragon, however, is not interested and goes back to sleep. The Wanderer leaves, and Alberich hides. At daybreak Siegfried arrives with Mime. Casting himself down under a tree to rest, Siegfried marvels at the calls of the birds, even fashioning himself a pipe to answer them (the beautiful 'Siegfried Idyll'). Then he blows a challenge to Fafner on his horn, and the dragon appears belching smoke. Siegfried drives the sword into the dragon's heart. The dying Fafner warns him of Mime's plot. As Siegfried withdraws his sword, some of the dragon's blood spills on his hand. In pain he puts his hand to his mouth and is suddenly able to understand the language of the birds, who inform him that he will be ruler of the world if he will take for himself the *tarnhelm* and ring. While he is getting them from the cave, Mime and Alberich engage in a quarrel about who shall have the magic objects. Mime plans to poison Siegfried when he returns, but Siegfried is warned by the bird and instead kills Mime with his sword. Then the bird promises to lead him to the most beautiful woman in the world, who can be won only by a hero who knows no fear. Siegfried leaves at once to seek her.

Act 3. begins in a wild spot near Brünnhilde's mountain. The Wanderer (Wotan) summons Erda to beg her to reveal the future, but she remains silent. Wotan tells her that he now sees the end of the gods, which she previously prophesied, and names Siegfried as his heir. He reveals that the hero will rescue Brünnhilde, who will redeem the world by her sacrifice. As Erda vanishes, Wotan goes to meet Siegfried, whose sword shatters Wotan's previously all-powerful spear. As Wotan falls back, Siegfried enters the flames which surround Brünnhilde.

Scene 2. takes place on top of the mountain where Brünnhilde lies asleep. In one of the musical highpoints of the opera, Siegfried removes the helmet of the sleeping warrior and is astonished by her beauty. He kisses her and she awakes. At first fearfully, then ardently, she returns Siegfried's passion, renouncing Valhalla for earthly love.

The final opera of the tetralogy is *Die Götterdämmerung* (*The Twilight of the Gods*). The prologue begins at Brünnhilde's rock at night. The three Norns (fates) are winding the rope of destiny. As they work, they tell Wotan's story and prophesy its ending. Finally their rope breaks, frayed by evil, and the Norns disappear. As dawn comes, Siegfried and Brünnhilde enter. Siegfried is in armour, and Brünnhilde is leading her horse Grane. He gives her the ring as a symbol of their love; in return, she gives him her horse. After a passionate farewell, he leaves on his journey.

Act 1. begins in the hall of the castle of Gibichungs on the Rhine. Gunther and his sister Gutrune are told by their half brother Hagen (the son of Alberich) that he has hopes of winning Siegfried for Gutrune and Brünnhilde for Gunther by means of a magic potion, which will cause Siegfried to forget that he ever loved Brünnhilde. When Siegfried arrives, he is warmly welcomed by the group, and Gutrune goes to prepare the potion. Hagen informs Siegfried of the powers of the *tarnhelm* (of which he was unaware), and Siegfried in turn reveals that he has left the ring on the hand of a woman. Gutrune hands the potion to Siegfried, and he at once forgets Brünnhilde and falls in love with Gutrune. It is arranged that he shall marry her in exchange for helping to woo Brünnhilde for Gunther, which, aided by the *tarnhelm*, he will do in Gunther's form. The two men mix their blood, swearing an oath of friendship, and leave on their quest. Hagen rejoices that they will surely bring him the ring.

Scene 2. takes place on Brünnhilde's rock. Waltraute, one of Brünnhilde's sisters, comes at Wotan's request to ask that she return the ring to the Rhinemaidens, thus removing the curse from the gods. She refuses to give up the ring, which for her is the symbol of Siegfried's love. Then Siegfried arrives wearing the *tarnhelm*, and in the guise of Gunther. Taking the ring from her, he claims her as Gunther's bride.

Act 2. begins on the banks of the Rhine near the Gibichungs' castle at night. Alberich convinces a half-sleeping Hagen to promise to get the ring for him. As day breaks Siegfried arrives to report his success, and a cheering chorus of vassals greet the arrival of Gunther and Brünnhilde. When she bitterly accuses Siegfried of betrayal, the hero is unperturbed and leaves happily with Gutrune. Now convinced of Siegfried's treachery, she confides to Hagen, who proposes to kill Siegfried, that he is only vulnerable in the back. Gunther, who wants the ring for himself, is persuaded to join them and suggests that they tell Gutrune that Siegfried was killed by a wild boar. The wedding procession enters, led by Siegfried and Gutrune. Brünnhilde and Gunther join them.

Act 3. begins in the woods near the Rhine. Having lost his way while hunting, Siegfried comes upon the Rhinemaidens. They beg him to return the ring to them, warning him of the curse, but he refuses and they swim off. Hunting horns are heard, and Hagen and Gunther enter with their kill as their vassals prepare a feast. Hagen hands Siegfried a cup of wine which contains a potion to restore his memory, and as Siegfried relates the story of his adventures, he remembers Brünnhilde. Two ravens fly overhead, and as he turns to watch them Hagen thrusts his spear into his back. His body is placed on his shield and the vassals bear it back to the castle.

Scene 2. takes place in the great hall of the Gibichungs' castle at night. Gutrune, seeing Siegfried's body, accuses her brother Gunther of murder, but he tells her that it was not he but rather Hagen who killed

Siegfried. Hagen admits his guilt and demands that he be given the ring as his reward. When Gunther refuses to agree, Hagen kills him. Then he goes to take the ring from Siegfried's dead hand, but to the horror of all the hand rises in warning. Meanwhile Brünnhilde has heard the complete story from the Rhinemaidens. She orders the vassals to prepare an enormous funeral pyre on the banks of the Rhine and to place Siegfried's body on it. She draws the ring from his finger, promising to return it to the Rhinemaidens after it has been purified by fire. Commanding the two messenger ravens to tell Loge to kindle the fire in Valhalla, she rides her horse onto the funeral pyre. The Rhine overflows its banks and the Rhinemaidens appear. Hagen, still grabbing for the ring, is borne off by Woglinde and Wellgunde, while Flosshilde triumphantly holds it above her head. In the distance Valhalla is enveloped in flames.

Three other operas belong to Wagner's mature period. *Tristan und Isolde* (1865) is Wagner's version of this great love legend from the Middle Ages. *Die Meistersinger von Nürnberg* (*The Mastersingers of Nuremberg* – 1868), Wagner's only excursion into comedy, tells the story of the

---

Birgit Nilsson (Swedish soprano, b. 1918), the well known Wagnerian singer, as Brünnhilde preparing to ride her horse into the funeral pyre. (Metropolitan Opera performance)

16th-century singing competition in Nuremberg, the winner of which wins the hand of a beautiful maid in marriage. *Parsifal* (1882), Wagner's last opera, deals with the medieval legend of the Holy Grail (the cup used by Christ at the Last Supper).

A friend and assistant of Wagner, Engelbert Humperdinck (1854–1921), wrote a charming opera based on the popular folktale for children, *Hänsel und Gretel*. The libretto was written by Humperdinck's sister, Adelheid Wette (1858–1916). Earlier Humperdinck had supplied music for a dramatic version of 'Snow White', which she had written for her children's puppet theatre. Her second play, with its delightful poetry, inspired Humperdinck to attempt something more elaborate in the way of a musical setting. For some time he had found himself living in the shadow of Wagner's idiosyncratic style, which was imitated by many other composers of the period. Only after Wagner's death did he feel enough trust in his own musical abilities to begin serious work on *Hänsel und Gretel*. He at first set the work as a *Singspiel* but later developed it into a through-composed work (one set to music throughout), which is the version performed today. The young composer Richard Strauss conducted the première in Weimar, Germany, on December 23, 1893.

The overture begins with the melody of the Children's Prayer from the end of the second act and also includes the themes of the Witch and the Dewman.

Act 1. begins in a shabby room, where Hänsel is making brooms and Gretel is knitting and singing an old German folksong (*Suse, liebe Suse – Susie, dear Susie*). Hänsel mockingly sings a second verse complaining of their hardships. Gretel tries to cheer him and persuades him to join her in a dance (*Brüderchen, komm tanz' mit mir – Little brother, come dance with me*). When their mother returns, she is angry with them for not working and reaches for a stick to beat them. In doing so she knocks over the pitcher of milk that was meant to be their supper. In a rage she orders Hänsel and Gretel to go and gather wild strawberries from the woods. After the children have gone, she sinks into a chair and falls into an exhausted sleep.

The children's father, a broommaker, is heard in the distance, singing a slightly drunken song as he comes home (*Ach, wir armen, armen Leute – Ah, we are poor, poor folk*), proclaiming that hunger is the best cook of all. He has managed to sell all his brooms at a good price and has brought home a huge basket of food. Both rejoice and dance around the room. Then her husband notices that the children are missing. When he hears that they have gone into the woods, he tells his wife that a witch lives there (*Eine Hex', steinalt, haust tief im Wald – A very old witch lives deep in the forest*), who lures children into her house and bakes them into gingerbread. In panic the two go out to search for their children.

106

The witch (Ann Howard) prepares Hänsel (Patricia Kern) for fattening-up in his cage. (Sadler's Wells Opera production)

Scene 2. takes place in the forest and is introduced by a prelude (*Hexenritt – The ride of the witches*). Gretel, who is weaving a garland of rose-hips while Hänsel looks for berries, sings a little folksong (*Ein Männlein steht im Walde – A little man stands in the wood*). When Hänsel's basket is full, the children play games and eat berries until it is quite dark. Hänsel admits that he does not know the way home, and Gretel is terrified by what she thinks is a ghost. As the children cower together in terror, the gentle Sandman (*Der kleine Sandmann bin ich – I am the little sandman*) tiptoes out of the forest gloom to throw sand in their sleepy eyes. Before they fall asleep, however, they sing their evening prayer (*Abends will ich schlafen gehn – In the evening I will go to sleep*), which tells of the fourteen angels who will come to guard them through the night. As they fall asleep, the angels enter quietly and arrange themselves protectively around the children.

Another prelude introduces Act 2. At dawn the Dewman (*Der kleine Taumann heiss' ich* – *I am called the little Dewman*) awakes Hänsel and Gretel by sprinkling them with dew. All is as it was the night before, except that a heavy mist now covers the ground. As it clears away they see behind them the Witch's gingerbread house. The hungry children creep forward to steal a bite. Suddenly they hear a voice calling out, '*Knusper, knusper, Knäuschen, wer knuspert mir am Häuschen?*' (*Nibble, nibble, little mousie, who is nibbling at my housie?*) The children answer that it is the wind and continue to eat. The Witch creeps out and throws a rope around Hänsel's neck. When the children try to run away, she puts a spell on them so that they cannot move. Hänsel is put in a cage to be fattened up for eating, and Gretel is sent to work in the kitchen. However, clever Gretel is able to break the spell on Hänsel by stealing the Witch's wand and repeating the magic words. Next she listens carefully as the Witch rides around the house on her broomstick, planning to get Gretel into the oven by asking her to put her head in to check the fire. When she is asked to do so, Gretel pretends to be extremely stupid and tells the Witch that she must show her how. Finally the exasperated Witch puts her own head in the oven, and Gretel, with Hänsel's help, is able to push her inside. The children dance around and rejoice at the Witch's death (*Juchnei! Nun ist die Hexe tot* – *Hurray, now the Witch is dead*). Suddenly the oven explodes, and the gingerbread falls off the gingerbread children who had formed the fence. Hänsel waves the Witch's wand, and the children join them in a dance (*Erlöst, befreit, für allezeit!* – *Delivered, freed forever!*).

The father enters with his happy song and joyfully greets his children. They now notice that the Witch herself has become gingerbread, and the father points out the moral of the story (*Kinder, schaut das Wunder an* – *Children, look at this marvellous thing*). Everyone joins him in the final line of the children's prayer: '*Wenn der Not aufs Höchste steigt, Gott der Herr die Hand uns reicht*' (*When our need is greatest, God the Lord gives us his hand*).

French Opera in the Second Half of the 19th Century – Gounod and Bizet

The two most popular French operas of the second half of the 19th century derived their inspiration not from the *grand opéra* but from the *opéra comique*. Both *Carmen* by Bizet and *Faust* by Gounod were originally composed with spoken dialogue, although later, for presentation at the prestigious Paris Opéra, both were through-composed (that is, arranged to be sung throughout).

Charles-François Gounod (1818–1893) wrote six operas, among them the popular story of *Faust*, which is based on a legend immortalized by the dramatic poem of Johann Wolfgang von Goethe (1749–1832). Part I of the poem, which contains the love story of Faust and Marguerite and on which Gounod based his opera, was published in German in 1808. Later it was translated into French prose (with some songs set in verse) by Gérard de Nerval. From this, Gounod's libretto was arranged by a team of professional librettists, Jules Barbier and Michel Carré. Other 19th-century composers who set this same story are Spohr (1816), Berlioz (1846) and Boïto (1868).

The original version of *Faust* was premièred at the Théâtre Lyrique in Paris on March 19, 1859. The through-composed version, which brought the opera popularity and which is most often heard today, was premièred at the Paris Opéra on March 3, 1869.

Although Gounod was accused at the time of 'Wagnerism', it is apparent from listening to the opera that the music is filled with lovely popular melodies, despite some use of *leitmotiv* and a declamatory style. It is written as a 'numbers opera', with clearly distinguishable arias.

The brief prelude contains a short fugue and also states the refrain of Valentin's second act aria, '*Avant de quitter ces lieux*'.

Act 1. takes place in the study of the aged scholar Faust in 16th-century Germany. Feeling that despite lifelong study, the meaning of existence still eludes him (*En vain j'interroge – In vain I ask*), he decides to poison himself but is distracted by the coming and going of humanity outside. Longing for renewed youth, he calls upon the Devil, who appears in the form of Méphistophélès. Encouraged by a vision of the beautiful Marguerite at her spinning wheel, Faust makes a bargain: on earth Méphistophélès will serve him; in hell he will serve Méphistophélès. Together the two sing of the joy that will now be Faust's (*A moi les plaisirs – For me the pleasures*).

Act 2. takes place in the village square. A fair is in progress, and many villagers are drinking and singing at a nearby inn (*Vin ou bière – Wine or beer*). Marguerite's soldier brother, Valentin, is leaving for war and is bidding farewell to his two friends: Wagner, a university student, and Siebel, who is in love with Marguerite. He reflects on the holy medal given him by his sister to guard him in battle and commends her to his friends' protection while he is away (*Avant de quitter ces lieux – Before I leave this place*). Wagner tries to raise his spirits with a silly drinking song (*Un rat plus poltron que brave – A rat more knave than brave*) but is interrupted by Méphistophélès, who sings his own song about how men worship gold (*Le veau d'or – The golden calf*). The students goodnaturedly

Edouard de Reszke (Polish bass, 1853–1917) as Méphistophélès proposing a toast in *Faust*. De Reszke first sang the role at Covent Garden in 1884, again at the Paris Opéra, and in 1903 at the Metropolitan, his final appearance before he retired to seclusion for many years, a victim of poverty and ill health.

join in on the refrain (*Et Satan conduit le bal – And Satan directs the dance*) and offer him a drink. In return, he tells their fortunes: Wagner will die at the beginning of the battle; Siebel will cause to wither any flower he henceforth touches; and Valentin will die by the hand of a man known to

Méphistophélès. Then Méphistophélès complains that the wine is terrible and suggests that they instead drink from the empty cask which is used as the tavern's sign. As he strikes the cask, the astonished students see wine pour out. Valentin objects when Méphistophélès proposes a toast to Marguerite, and the wine bursts into flame. The students and Valentin draw their swords, but Méphistophélès draws a circle around himself on the ground through which they cannot strike. Fearing enchantment, the group arranges their swords in the form of a cross (*De l'enfer qui vient émousser nos armes – When Hell attacks our weapons*), and, as Méphistophélès mocks them, they leave.

Faust enters looking for the girl of the vision and is reassured by Méphistophélès that she will arrive soon. The townspeople return (*Ainsi que la brise légère – Just as the gentle breeze*), followed by Marguerite. Faust goes over to her and offers her his arm, but she turns away from him.

Act 3. begins in Marguerite's garden. Siebel sings of his love for her, begging his flowers to speak for him (*Faites-lui mes aveux – Carry my vows*). All the flowers that he touches wither, until he dips his fingers in holy water. He then gathers a large bouquet and places them at Marguerite's door. Méphistophélès and Faust observe this, and Méphistophélès suggests that he can supply Faust with a better gift for Marguerite. Faust, alone, sings of his love for her (*Salut! demeure chaste et pure – Hail! Chaste and pure dwelling*). Méphistophélès returns with a jewel case, which they leave by Marguerite's door. She comes into the garden and sits down to spin. While she works, she sings the ballad of the King of Thule, punctuating her song with reflections on the handsome stranger who accosted her in the square. As she rises, she notices the flowers and then the jewel case. Opening it, she is amazed by the contents and begins to try them on, singing the famous and brilliant 'Jewel Song' (*Je ris de me voir – I smile to see myself*). Marthe, a neighbour, arrives and is admiring the jewels as Faust and Méphistophélès enter. Méphistophélès distracts Marthe by telling her that her husband is dead, and Faust and Marguerite are left together. They reveal their love for each other, but Marguerite runs away when Faust tries to embrace her. Méphistophélès, who has disposed of Marthe, returns to gloat over the coming downfall of Marguerite (*O nuit, étends sur eux ton ombre! – O night, let your shadow fall on them!*). Faust and Marguerite return to the garden to bid each other good night. Faust remains in the garden, and soon Marguerite appears at her window. He rushes to her and the lovers embrace.

Act 4. begins in Marguerite's room. As she spins, she sadly sings that Faust has deserted her (*Il ne revient pas – He will not return*). Only Siebel remains to comfort her (*Si le bonheur à sourire t'invite – If fortune invites you to smile*). She tells him that she will go to church to pray for her lover and for the child whom she is going to bear him.

111

Scene 2. takes place in the church. As Marguerite tries to pray, a chorus of demons call her name. Méphistophélès appears from a tomb to warn her that she is damned, and as she desperately continues to pray, he repeats that she is doomed.

Scene 3. takes place on the street near the church. Valentin and his fellow soldiers have returned from war. Eagerly he asks Siebel about Marguerite, but Siebel evades his questions. He vainly tries to prevent Valentin from entering Marguerite's cottage, and as she leaves she begs him to have pity on his sister. Méphistophélès enters and prompts Faust to sing an insulting parody of a serenade (*Vous qui faites l'endormie* – *You who pretend to sleep*) under Marguerite's window. Valentin comes out to protect Marguerite's honour with his sword, angrily throwing away the holy medal she gave him before he left for war. He challenges Faust to a duel and is mortally wounded. Marthe and the villagers arrive to find him dying. When Marguerite comes to him, begging his forgiveness, he curses her and dies.

Act 5. usually begins in a prison where Marguerite awaits death for killing her baby. Faust and Méphistophélès enter to find her asleep. She awakes upon hearing Faust's voice, but believes herself to be dreaming and cannot respond to his demands for her to leave with him. Instead she begins to pray (*Anges purs, anges radieux* – *Pure angels, radiant angels*). Suddenly she asks Faust why his hands are stained with blood and orders him to leave her. As she dies the prison walls open and her soul ascends to heaven accompanied by a choir of angels.

Gounod wrote five other operas, of which *Mireille* (1864) and *Roméo et Juliette* (1867) are sometimes performed today.

The most popular French opera of the second half of the 19th century is undoubtedly *Carmen*, by Georges Bizet (1838–1875). Bizet was brought up by two musical parents and entered the conservatory at the age of nine. Like Berlioz he had difficulty getting his operas performed.

The libretto for *Carmen* was written by a team of librettists, Henri Meilhac and Ludovic Halévy, following a short novel by Prosper Mérimée (1845). *Carmen* had been a scandalous success as a book, and the libretto, although toned down in several respects, was still considered shocking by many, for its sordid ending and the realism with which Carmen's self-centred character is presented were unusual at the time.

Like Gounod, Bizet was accused of 'Wagnerism' and also of writing 'untuneful' music. Perhaps the music of *Carmen* sounded unmelodic to French ears accustomed to Meyerbeer, but it sounds unquestionably melodic from the perspective of the 20th century. Bizet did employ the concept of *leitmotiv* in a very limited way, but his use of thematic relationships within the opera is more like Verdi's approach than Wagner's. Echoes of Spanish local colour are reflected in the exciting

The bullfighter Escamillo (Geoffrey Chard) looks admiringly at the flirtatious Carmen (Ann Howard). (English National Opera production)

rhythms and orchestration of *Carmen*.

Carmen was originally written as an *opéra comique*. An unusual feature is that the dialogue is often spoken over a musical accompaniment. At a later date music was composed for recitatives by Bizet's friend Ernest Guiraud to make the work conform to the standards of the Paris Opéra, but this version is rarely performed today. The opera was begun in 1872 and was premièred at the Opéra Comique in Paris on March 3, 1875.

The brilliant prelude is composed of themes from the opera, including Carmen's 'destiny' theme, which is cut off by a single dramatic chord.

Act 1. takes place in a square in Seville, which is filled with soldiers and

Marilyn Horne (American mezzo-soprano, b. 1934) as the gypsy
Carmen.

townspeople. Micaela enters, looking for her sweetheart, Don José.
Morales, an army officer, suggests that she wait until Don José arrives at
the guardhouse, but she prefers to return later. The relief guard marches
in followed by a crowd of children, who imitate them, and Zuniga (a
captain) and Don José (a corporal) take up their posts. From a nearby
cigarette factory, working girls released by the noon bell enter the plaza.
With them is the attractive gypsy Carmen. As the men begin to flirt with
her, she responds by warning them that love cannot be tamed, in the
famous dance-like 'Habañera' (*L'amour est un oiseau rebelle* – *Love is a
rebellious bird*). Noticing José, who is pointedly ignoring her, she throws
him a flower (as her theme sounds in the orchestra) and runs away. José is

left alone with the flower. Micaela enters to bring him a message and some money from his mother. Together they sing sentimentally of their childhood home (*Ma mère, je la vois – I see my mother*), but the duet is interrupted by Carmen's theme as José ponders whether Micaela's arrival has saved him from an evil fate. She leaves him to read his mother's letter, and he promises himself that he will marry Micaela and forget the girl who threw him the flower. But a fight breaks out in the factory, and soon an insolent Carmen is led out by Zuniga and turned over to José to be locked up. Alone with him, she taunts him with his love for her and teasingly sings the 'Seguidilla' (*Près des remparts de Séville – Near the walls of Seville*), suggesting that she knows a place where she might meet a new lover. By the time Zuniga returns with the order to imprison her, José has been won over, and together they plan a way for her to escape.

After a brief instrumental *entr'acte* (a piece of music performed between the acts), Act 2. takes place in an inn outside the walls of Seville. Gypsies are dancing, and officers and smugglers are sitting at tables. Carmen and her friends, Frasquita and Mercedes, begin a song about the gypsies' love of gaiety (*Les tringles des sistres tintaient – The bells of the tambourines jingle*). Zuniga reveals to Carmen in passing that José was sent to prison for allowing her to escape, but that he has now been released. An admiring crowd enters with Escamillo, a famous bullfighter, who describes his triumph in the ring in the swaggering 'Toreador Song' (*Votre toast . . . je peux vous le rendre – I am able to return your toast*). He then joins the circle of Carmen's admirers, who are trying to persuade her to join them in a smuggling venture. She refuses, saying that she intends to wait for José. He is first heard offstage in a brief unaccompanied air (*Halt là! Qui va là! – Halt! Who goes there!*). He joins Carmen, who dances for him, but when the bugle sounds, ordering his return to camp, he tells her he must leave. She mocks him, saying that it is clear he does not love her. Stung by her words, he responds in a passionate aria, the 'Flower Song' (*La fleur que tu m'avais jetée – The flower you threw to me*), which is introduced by Carmen's theme. Still unwilling to desert the army, he is preparing to leave when the jealous Zuniga bursts in and picks a quarrel. José draws his sword, and the gypsies seize Zuniga. It is now impossible for José to return to camp, and he reluctantly agrees to join the smugglers. They conclude the act by singing of the joys of a gypsy life.

After another *entr'acte*, Act 3. takes place at the smugglers' camp in the mountains, where José is lamenting that he has broken faith with his mother. Carmen is watching as Mercedes and Frasquita tell their fortunes, and she comments to José that his fate is revealed in the cards, and there is nothing, after all, that he can do about it. Then she reads her own fortune and discovers that the cards reveal only death.

After the smugglers have moved on, Micaela enters, again looking for

José. In her aria (*Je dis que rien ne m'épouvante* – *I tell myself that nothing frightens me*) she prays for God's help in facing the woman who has destroyed the man she loves. Escamillo arrives, looking for Carmen, and picks a fight with José. The toreador is wounded in the clash but saved from death by Carmen's intervention. As he leaves he ironically invites them all to his forthcoming bullfight in Seville. Micaela finds José and begs him to return with her to his mother, who is dying. As he leaves, he warns Carmen that they will meet again.

After a strongly rhythmic *entr'acte*, Act 4. takes place in a square in Seville near the bullring. A huge crowd of men, women and children collect to talk, peddle their wares and dance. Escamillo arrives with Carmen, to the cheers of the crowd. Mercedes and Frasquita warn her to leave, for they have seen José, but Carmen is unintimidated and plans to meet him. As the crowd enters the amphitheatre, Carmen and José remain behind. He begs for her love, but she refuses him, and, as sudden applause rings out from the amphitheatre, she turns to leave him. In despair he blocks her way, demanding to know if she now loves Escamillo. She responds by angrily telling him to kill her or to let her go. As she tries to run into the amphitheatre, he catches her and stabs her. The crowd pours out, cheering Escamillo, as José laments that he has killed the woman he loves.

One other opera of Bizet is occasionally performed: *Les Pêcheurs de Perles* (*The Pearl Fishers* – 1863).

Several other noted French composers of opera followed Bizet. Camille Saint-Saëns (1835–1921) is remembered for *Samson et Dalila* (1877), and Jules Massenet (1842–1912) for *Manon* (1884) and *Thaïs* (1894). Claude Debussy (1862–1918), wrote a dream-like, lyric and impressionistic opera, *Pelléas et Mélisande* (1902), taking as his libretto a play by the same name (1892) by Maurice Maeterlinck (1862–1949), the Belgian symbolist poet and playwright.

Nationalist Opera in the Slavonic Countries

During the last half of the 19th century, independent musical traditions began to arise in countries that had previously been dominated by imported musical styles from France, Italy or Germany. This trend towards national schools of composition led many composers in the Slavonic countries to incorporate their native folk music into their operas and to choose as subjects various patriotic and national themes. Several of these works have found a place in the international operatic repertory.

Among these operas is *The Bartered Bride* (*Prodaná Nevěsta*) by Bedřich Smetana (1824–1884), who is considered to be the father of Czech

(Bohemian) national music. Of his eight operas, only this one has achieved an international reputation. Smetana had begun his career as a composer by writing in a strongly Germanic style, but eventually he turned to the music of his own country. *The Bartered Bride*, premièred on May 30, 1866, at the National Theatre in Prague, is entitled a 'Folk Opera', although it contains no actual folk melodies. The style of composition is strongly influenced by Bohemian folk music, however, not only in melody but in the strongly marked dance rhythms it contains. In its original form as a *Singspiel* in two acts, it was not exceptionally successful, possibly because the première took place during the war between Austria and Prussia when Prague expected to be occupied at any moment. Recitatives were composed for the performance which took place on September 25, 1870, in Prague, and this time the opera was a great success. A performance in Vienna in 1892 in a German translation brought the work international attention and began a tradition of German productions (*Die Verkaufte Braut*) which is maintained to this day. The characters were given new names at this point: Mařenka = Marie; Wašek = Wenzel; Jeník = Hans; Ludmila = Kathinka; Háta = Agnes.

The lively overture presents themes from choruses in the opera. Act 1. takes place on the village green of a small Bohemian town. It is the annual spring feastday of the parish church, and the villagers are celebrating. Hans and Marie, who are in love, are talking together as the villagers drift off. Marie has been told by her parents that a marriage has been arranged for her – to Wenzel, the half-witted son of the wealthy farmer Tobias Micha. Marie is suspicious of Hans' apparent lack of concern at her news, but he is able to reassure her. In an aria (*Gern ja will ich Dir vertrauen – Gladly will I trust you*) she tells him that without him she would be lost. She then asks why he never mentions his home and family. Hans tells her that his family is quite wealthy, but after his mother's death, his father remarried, and his stepmother, who disliked him, was able to convince his father to send him away. In the following duet (*Mit der Mutter sank zu Grabe – When my mother was laid in her grave*) Marie sympathizes with Hans' misfortune, and the two plan a happier life together. Seeing Kezal, the marriage broker, approaching with Marie's parents, Kruschina and Kathinka, Hans leaves and Marie hides. Despite the doubts of Marie's parents, Kezal insists that 'Everything is as good as settled' (*Alles ist so gut wie richtig*) for Marie's marriage to Wenzel: he is Micha's only living son and a very good catch indeed (*Gekommen wär' er mit mir wie gerne – He would willingly have come with me*). Marie joins the group and tells them that she is pledged to another. Her parents then suggest to Kezal that it would be a good idea for Wenzel himself to speak to Marie, and Kezal very reluctantly agrees. Villagers again fill the green and the act ends with a happy chorus.

117

After the strong man impresses the crowd, the ballerina on the left casually picks up the 500-pound weight and walks off with it, in a scene from *The Bartered Bride*.

Act 2. takes place inside the inn, where the villagers are drinking and singing. Hans and Kezal have a difference of opinion on the relative value of love and money. The village girls appear, inviting the men to come dance with them, and all leave together. A most unhappy Wenzel enters, stuttering that his mother has ordered him to go to court a girl (*Theu . . . theu . . . theurer Sohn – De . . . de . . . dearest son*). Marie, whom he has never seen, follows him in and persuades him to refuse to marry 'Marie', because another girl (herself) likes him so very much (*Ich weiss Euch einen lieben Schatz – I know of a little sweetheart for you*).

They leave, and Kezal enters with Hans, whom he tries to convince to renounce Marie. In duet (*Weiss ich doch Eine – I know a girl*), Kezal tries to sell Hans on the idea of a rich marriage, and Hans pretends to be interested. Finally Kezal offers Hans money to break off with Marie. Hans agrees and a contract is drawn up with the stipulation that Marie may marry only the son of Tobias Micha. As Kezal leaves, Hans remarks that he has trapped the man. Then he sings of his love for Marie and of his hope that they will soon be wed (*Es muss gelingen* – *It must succeed*). The villagers enter with Kezal, who reads them the contract. In astonishment they watch Hans sign away his bride, as Marie's father witnesses the document.

Act 3. takes place on the green. Wenzel enters singing of his courtship difficulties: the girl he hopes to marry has disappeared (*O, was ich mich be trü . . . trübe* – *O how tr . . . troubled I am*). A circus arrives, advertising a dancing bear, who is to perform with the charming Esmerelda. The 'bear' doesn't turn up, for he has had too much to drink at the local inn. Springer, the circus manager, asks Wenzel to take his place. Delighted, Wenzel agrees and is taught his steps by the manager and Esmerelda (*Alles geht am Schnürchen* – *Everything's going like clockwork*). When they leave, Wenzel remains behind to practise. He is discovered by Kezal, Micha and Agnes (Micha's wife), who tell him that he must sign the contract to marry Marie. He refuses and runs off, leaving the three angrily making plans to bring him to his senses (*Das sind verwünschte Dinge* – *That's a cursed thing*). Marie, mourning over the story of Hans' deceit, enters with her parents. Wenzel then returns, recognizes Marie as the girl who had flirted with him earlier and agrees to marry her, much to the relief of Kezal and Wenzel's parents. Marie, however, will not agree to accept Wenzel's hand at once and asks for a moment alone in which to consider the matter. In a sextet (*Noch ein Weilchen, Marie* – *A little longer, Marie*), all remind her that she should think carefully before rejecting such a good offer.

Alone, Marie sings sadly of her betrayal (*Wie fremd und tot is Alles umher* – *How strange and dead is everything around*). Hans enters to tell her that everything was a joke, but she can no longer trust him. When Kezal returns to ask Marie if she will agree to marry Micha's son, Hans says that she certainly shall. Marie angrily orders him to leave her, as both sets of parents arrive, followed by the villagers. Hans is immediately recognized by Micha and Agnes as their long lost son. He turns to Marie and asks her to choose between Wenzel and himself as a bridegroom, and Marie throws herself into his arms, as everyone laughs at Kezal. The circus arrives and Wenzel, dressed as the bear, frightens everyone until he is unmasked. The parents bless the marriage and the opera concludes with a joyous chorus.

Overleaf: The 'bear' frightens the villagers before being unmasked. (Covent Garden, 1955)

The Czech operatic tradition begun by Smetana was continued by Leoš Janáček (1854–1928), whose *Jenufa* (1904), *Káta Kabanová* (1921), *The Cunning Little Vixen* (1924), *The Makropulos Case* (1926), and *From the House of the Dead* (1930) gradually have gained an international audience.

In Russia, opera began as a largely Italian enterprise under Catherine the Great (1762–1796), who imported not only Italian operas but also Italian opera composers to her court at St Petersburg (now Leningrad). In fact, the first opera written in the Russian language was composed by an Italian, Catterino Cavos (1775–1840).

Mikhail Ivanovich Glinka (1804–1857) was the first native-born Russian composer of opera. Writing in a basically Italianate style, he also included some of the elements of Russian folk music in his compositions. He had a great influence on later Russian composers, who were particularly drawn to the great choral scenes of his operas. *Russlan and Ludmilla* (1842) and *A Life for the Czar* (1836) are his best known works.

Following in Glinka's footsteps were a group of five Russian composers dedicated to the development of a Russian national musical style. This group, variously described by historians as 'the Russian five' or 'the mighty handful', was made up of Balakirev, Cui, Moussorgsky, Borodin and Rimsky-Korsakov. The last three of these composers are known for their operas. Alexander Porfirievich Borodin (1833–1887) is the composer of *Prince Igor* (1890), which contains the famous Polovtsian dances. Nicolai Andreyevich Rimsky-Korsakov wrote a considerable number of operas, many of which are based on fairytales. Among these are *Sadko* (1898), *The Legend of the Invisible City of Kitezh* (1907) and *The Golden Cockerel* (1909).

The best known of this group is Modest Petrovich Moussorgsky (1839–1881). His *Boris Godunov* is widely considered to be the greatest Russian opera, and the part of Boris is certainly the greatest bass role in all operatic literature. The libretto, arranged by the composer himself, follows the story of the same name by the great Russian poet Alexander Pushkin (1799–1837). Like many national operas, a historical subject is the plot – in this case the reign of the usurper Czar Boris (1598–1605). Boris Godunov, a member of the court of Czar Feodor, is supposed to have arranged the murder of Feodor's younger brother Dimitri, the heir to the throne, although the historical evidence on this point is extremely weak. When Feodor died, Boris achieved his own selection as Czar through the forced support of the Russian people. A young novice, Grigory (the 'false Dimitri'), who had fled to Poland, reappeared in Russia claiming to be Dimitri, the brother of Czar Feodor, and organized a revolution which led to the deposition of Boris.

Moussorgsky's musical style employs a powerful recitative, with irregular phrases and modal melodies. There are few traditionally structured arias. The opera is composed of a series of detached units or tableau scenes. This is a characteristic of Russian art forms and can also be seen in the episodic structure of Leo Tolstoy's novel *War and Peace* (1865–69), as well as in Moussorgsky's own set of piano pieces, *Pictures at an Exhibition* (1874).

Many versions exist of this famous opera. *Boris* was first written in 1868–69 and was extensively revised in 1871–72 before its première performance at the Maryinsky Theatre in St Petersburg on February 8, 1874. In 1896 the score was edited by Rimsky-Korsakov, and a second edition in 1908 achieved international success for the work. In 1928 the two original versions of the score were printed. In 1941 Dimitri Shostakovitch (1906–1975) revised the opera yet again, giving special attention to the orchestration. It is possible to see almost any of these versions in performance today. As a result the order of the scenes may vary from production to production, and the act divisions also may occur at different points. The popular Rimsky-Korsakov edition is outlined here. Today most performances are in Russian, although at one time it was not unusual to hear it done in one of the more common languages of opera, such as German or Italian, or even in a combination of languages – the principals singing in Russian, and the chorus in German, for example.

The prelude begins in the courtyard of a monastery near Moscow, where Russian peasants have been organized by the police to beg Boris, who retired here after Feodor's death, to accept the throne. A group of boyars (nobles) enter the monastery and soon, Andrei Shchelkalov, secretary of the duma (council), comes out of the monastery to announce that Russia is doomed, for Boris refuses to accept the throne. A procession of pilgrims arrives and enters the monastery, and the peasants are dispersed with orders to reappear at the Kremlin in Moscow the following day.

Scene 2. of the prelude takes place in the courtyard of the Kremlin in Moscow, which is surrounded by great churches. Accompanied by the tolling of the great church bells, Boris' coronation procession leaves the Cathedral of the Assumption as the people cheer. Despite this show of support, Boris is troubled and pauses to pray that his reign will be a good one. The procession moves on.

Act 1. begins in the monastery cell of the monk Pimen. While the novice Grigory sleeps, Pimen writes his chronicle of Russia's history. Grigory is awakened by a recurring nightmare in which he dreams that he has climbed into a high tower which is surrounded by a crowd of mocking people. As he grows calmer, he laments that, unlike Pimen, who fought as a soldier and saw the magnificent court of Ivan the Terrible, he has lived all his life in the monastery. Remembering the

Feodor Ivanovich Chaliapin (Russian bass-baritone, 1873–1938) as
Boris Godunov. A peasant's son, Chaliapin became one of the
most celebrated Russian basses and singing actors, with his
flashing eyes and dramatic appearance.

glorious days of the past, Pimen comments that they now live under
the rule of a murderer. He had hoped to record the reign of the young
prince Dimitri, who, had he lived, would now be of Grigory's age.
Instead he is forced to record the infamous reign of Boris. But Grigory
predicts that even Boris will not escape judgement.

Scene 2. takes place in an inn near the Lithuanian border, where the
Hostess is singing a lively song as she works. Missail and Varlaam, two
wandering monks, enter with Grigory to beg some silver to build a
church. After a drinking song about Czar Ivan's battle with the Tartars in
Kazan, the two monks fall asleep, while Grigory goes to speak to the
Hostess. She mentions that there are border guards on the main road to

Lithuania, but that they will never catch the man for whom they wait since he will surely use a secret path which she points out to Grigory. Soldiers arrive searching for Grigory, with a warrant containing his description. The officer in charge cannot read, so Grigory reads out the warrant, changing the description to fit Varlaam. Varlaam grabs the paper, and although he can spell words out only with difficulty, he discovers that the description is that of Grigory. At that Grigory draws a knife and leaves through the window.

Act 2., set in Boris' apartments in the Kremlin, begins as a picture of domestic tranquillity. Xenia, Boris' daughter, and Feodor, his son, are there with their nurse. Xenia is weeping over a picture of her dead fiancé, and the nurse is making an unsuccessful attempt to cheer her with a silly song. Feodor has more luck by starting a clapping game in which the others join. Boris enters to greet his children with affection. After Xenia and the nurse leave, he discusses geography briefly with his son, but then he seems to fall into a trance in which he sings that despite his peaceful rule the murdered child has destroyed his happiness. A commotion is heard outside, and Boris sends Feodor to discover what has happened. In his absence a boyar enters to tell Boris that Prince Shuisky desires to speak with him. He whispers that Shuisky and some others are plotting against the Czar. In this connection a messenger arrived the previous night from Poland. Boris orders the arrest of the messenger and agrees to see Shuisky. Feodor then returns to explain that the cause of the disturbance was the children's parakeet, which nipped the ears of the servants with its beak. Touched by the story, Boris embraces his son. Shuisky enters, and despite the fact that Boris greets him with insults, he reports to him that the false Dimitri has escaped into Lithuania. Asking his son to leave them, Boris first orders Shuisky to arrange to guard the border against his return and then demands from him confirmation that the real Dimitri was indeed killed. Shuisky replies that he himself saw the body of the child as it lay in the cathedral for five days after the murder. Boris then asks Shuisky to leave him. Alone, he imagines that he sees the dead child approaching him, and he prays and begs the child to have mercy on him and leave him.

Act 3. begins in the room of Marina Mnishek in the Polish castle of Sandomir, owned by her wealthy father. Bored with her ladies-in-waiting, she dismisses them and sings of her new interest, the young Dimitri, who she hopes will overthrow Boris and rule Russia with her as his queen. Rangoni, a Jesuit, comes to persuade Marina that it is her religious duty to ensnare Dimitri with her beauty and convince him to reject Russian Orthodoxy for Roman Catholicism, thus winning all Russia for the Catholic Church. [The Russians' Orthodoxy and the Poles' Catholicism have been a source of conflict throughout the history of the two countries.] Marina refuses until Rangoni threatens her with damnation. In terror she submits.

Scene 2. takes place in the gardens of the castle. Alone, Dimitri sings of his love for Marina, who has promised to meet him at midnight. Rangoni enters to tell him that Marina loves him deeply and that because of this her reputation has suffered. Dimitri vows to make her his queen and thus to confound the gossips. They hide as a group of ladies and gentlemen enter to discuss how the Polish forces will overcome the armies of Russia and take Moscow. Marina offers wine to the group as they enter the castle, and they toast her as the future Queen of Russia. Soon Marina returns to meet Dimitri. She taunts him with his failure to begin the fight against Boris. Only when he angrily promises to lead an immediate attack does she tell him that she loves him.

Act 4. begins in a forest clearing near the town of Kromy, close to Moscow. Peasants enter, dragging with them the boyar Krushchov, a captured supporter of Boris, and begin to mock him. They are distracted from this by the arrival of a simpleton, followed by a crowd of young boys who are tormenting him. [In Russia there was a common folk belief that these simpletons had the gift of prophecy or special wisdom.] Next the monks Varlaam and Missail arrive to urge the crowd to accept Dimitri, the lawful heir to the throne, in place of Boris. Two Jesuit priests cause another diversion as they arrive singing in Latin. At once the peasants, encouraged by the monks, bind them and take them away. Next a procession enters, led by the false Dimitri on horseback. The crowd welcomes him with cheers, and he promises them and even Krushchov pardon and protection. He leaves, followed by the crowd, and the simpleton is left alone to mourn the fate of Russia.

Scene 2. takes place in the council room of the Kremlin, where the duma is holding an emergency session to discuss the rebellion against Boris. Shuisky tells them that he fears for Boris' sanity: He had lingered to observe Boris' behaviour after being dismissed by him the previous day, and saw Boris speaking to the ghost of the dead child Dimitri. Boris enters in a rage, and Shuisky begs permission to call in an old monk to speak to the council about a most important matter. Pimen enters with a remarkable story: A shepherd, blind from birth, has had his sight restored at the tomb of the child Dimitri, and at the instant he regained his vision, he saw in front of him the living Dimitri. Boris collapses into the arms of the boyars, and, realizing that he is dying, commands them to bring to him his son Feodor and to leave them alone. He bids his son farewell, asking him to care for his sister and to rule well and justly. He prays that God will guard him and his throne. The death bell begins to toll, and the monks begin to chant offstage. A group of boyars and monks return to the room to hear Boris name Feodor as the new Czar.

A scene at the country house of Madame Larina. Lensky (centre) is
played by Nicolai Gedda in a Metropolitan Opera performance.

Muttering 'forgive me' under his breath, he sinks into his chair and dies.

A contemporary of Moussorgsky was Peter Ilyich Tchaikovsky
(1840–1893), perhaps the most famous of Russian composers.
Tchaikovsky wrote *Eugene Onegin* to a libretto taken by Konstantin
Shilovsky from Alexander Pushkin's novel in verse of the same name.
Just as *Boris Godunov* assumes that the audience will have a certain
knowledge of Russian history, this opera assumes a knowledge of the
Pushkin novel, which was extremely popular in Russia. Unlike *Boris
Godunov*, which was written for an enormous stage, *Onegin* has the more
personal dimensions of a chamber opera. In fact it was described by the
composer not as an opera, but as 'lyric scenes'. Its first performance at the
Maly Theatre in Moscow on March 29, 1879, by students from
the Moscow Conservatory conveyed the intimacy that the composer

desired. Tchaikovsky's elegant and graceful music reinforces the air of gentle melancholy that pervades this work.

After a short prelude based on Tatyana's wistful theme, Act 1. begins in the garden of the Larins' country estate. Mme. Larina, a widow, and Filippyevna, Tatyana's old nurse, are making jam on a portable stove while they reminisce about the past. Tatyana and Olga, Mme. Larina's daughters, sing a love song in duet. A group of peasants arrives, bringing a decorated sheaf of hay as tribute, and Mme. Larina asks them to perform some traditional songs and dances. Olga dances a few steps too, but Tatyana is too absorbed in her book, which relates the trials and tribulations of two lovers, to respond. Her mother – expressing a theme that runs throughout the opera – warns her that the romance in the book is not at all like real life, in which there are no heroes. Vladimir Lensky, a young poet and landowner who is Olga's fiancé, arrives with his friend, Eugene Onegin, whom he introduces to Tatyana. Tatyana is immediately impressed with Onegin, and for his part he cannot understand why Lensky should prefer Olga. Lensky and Olga wander off together, leaving Tatyana and Onegin to a brief discussion of books and dreams. When they in turn leave, Lensky returns to sing to Olga of his love for her. As darkness falls, the young people go in for dinner, leaving Filippyevna shaking her head at the realization that Tatyana has fallen in love with Onegin.

Scene 2. takes place in Tatyana's room. While Tatyana prepares for bed, she asks Filippyevna to tell of her own marriage. Filippyevna explains that it was most unromantic: her marriage was arranged when she was very young, and one did not consider love in those days. Finally Tatyana, bidding her nurse goodnight, confesses that she herself is in love. She cannot sleep, however, and decides to write to Onegin to tell him of her love. As this famous 'letter scene' draws to a close dawn is breaking. Filippyevna bustles into the room, and Tatyana persuades her to make arrangements for delivering the letter.

Scene 3. takes place in the garden, where peasant girls are singing. As they leave, Onegin enters to speak with Tatyana, who is nervously awaiting him. Politely but coldly he tells her that he was much touched by her letter, but that he can feel for her only a brother's love. As the care-free voices of the peasant girls are heard again in the distance, he advises her to learn greater self-control. He courteously offers her his arm and together they return to the house.

Act 2. begins in the ballroom of Mme. Larina's house. Elegantly dressed men and women are dancing and talking together. Onegin asks Tatyana to dance, but then, bored, he turns his attention to Olga. Seeing that Lensky is annoyed by this, Onegin begins to flirt outrageously with her. Jealously Lensky reproaches Olga, who merely laughs at him. The

The challenge in the ballroom. Students from the Moscow conservatory in the first performance of *Eugene Onegin* in 1879.

incipient quarrel is interrupted by the arrival of Triquet, an elderly French tutor who, in a fine comic scene, reads some interminable French verses in honour of Tatyana. The storm between Lensky and Onegin has not passed, however, and Lensky continues to condemn his friend's behaviour. Finally he challenges Onegin to a duel, and bidding farewell to Olga he rushes out.

Scene 2. takes place on the banks of a river on an early winter morning. Lensky and Zaretsky, his second, are waiting for Onegin. As Zaretsky walks off, Lensky sings regretfully of his happy past and has a premonition of his approaching death. Zaretsky returns to announce the arrival of Onegin and his second, Guillot. As the seconds discuss the arrangements for the duel, Lensky and Onegin sing a duet: both meditate on stopping the insane course that events have taken, but neither is willing to turn back. They move to their places. Onegin fires and Lensky falls to the ground.

Act 3. begins in the ballroom of an elegant house in St Petersburg. Onegin enters, bored with his empty life. He has killed his best friend and cannot find satisfaction in work or find a wife. Around him a dance begins. At its conclusion, Prince Gremin enters with his lovely wife Tatyana, who does not at once recognize Onegin. Onegin does not immediately recognize Tatyana either, although he is immensely impressed with her grace and asks Gremin to present him to her. The Prince agrees to this, informing Onegin in a moving bass aria that Tatyana is his wife, his whole life, who means everything to him. When Onegin is presented to her, Tatyana favours him with some small talk and then asks her husband to take her home. As they leave, Onegin suddenly realizes that he loves her.

Scene 2. takes place in a room in Prince Gremin's house. Tatyana once again is awaiting Onegin, who has written her to beg an interview. He enters and throws himself at her feet, declaring his love. Asking him to rise, she reminds him of their earlier meeting in the garden after her letter to him. She admits that she still loves him, but she firmly tells him that she intends to be true to her husband who loves her. She asks him to leave, and when he does not obey, she walks out of the room. He remains alone, convinced that death is now his only hope.

Tchaikovsky wrote seven other operas, of which the dramatic *Queen of Spades* (*Pique-Dame* – 1890), to a libretto also taken from a work by Pushkin, is the most popular.

Several other Russian composers of note have contributed to the 20th-century opera repertory. Igor Stravinsky (1882–1971), who left Russia as a young man and composed in many countries and in many styles, is known for *Oedipus Rex* (1927) and *The Rake's Progress* (1951). Working in Russia were Sergei Prokofiev (1891–1953), whose most popular operas are *The Love for Three Oranges* (1921) and *War and Peace* (1946); and Dmitri Shostakovitch (1906–1975), who wrote *Lady Macbeth of Minsk* (1934).

Italian Opera after Verdi – Mascagni, Leoncavallo and Puccini

A new type of opera, called *verismo* (naturalism), appeared in Italy toward the end of the 19th century. To some extent a reaction against the musical domination of Verdi and Wagner, it was also related to the

Alfio the carter sings of his love for his beautiful (and faithless) wife Lola.

literary movement of 'naturalism' (as opposed to 'romanticism'), which presented scenes and characters from common life rather than the idealized figures of the earlier part of the century. The plots of *verismo* operas are characteristically fast moving, violent and sensational, with little elaboration or 'filler' material. Many elements of the style appeared in Bizet's *Carmen* fifteen years before the first Italian *verismo* opera was premièred, but there appears to be no direct line of descent from the earlier work.

Pietro Mascagni (1863–1945) is credited with the first opera in this style, *Cavalleria rusticana* (*Rustic Chivalry*), which was composed for a competition in only eight days. The libretto was written by Giovanni Targioni-Tozzetti and Guido Menasci after a very successful one-act play of the same name by the Sicilian novelist Giovanni Verga (1840–1922). Composed in a strong, primitive and very melodic style, the opera throws a harsh light on the violent events of an Easter Day in Sicily. The première performance took place at the Teatro Costanzi in Rome on May 17, 1890. An immediate success, the opera was performed in both England and the United States during the following year.

The prelude contains many of the major musical themes of the opera. It is interrupted by an offstage aria, a 'Siciliana', accompanied by harp. Turridu, a young soldier, is singing of the charms of Lola, to whom he was betrothed before he left to serve in the army. During his absence, however, Lola proved fickle and is now married to Alfio, a teamster.

Bells are ringing as the curtain rises on the church square of a Sicilian village on Easter Day. At the side of the stage is the tavern kept by Turridu's mother, Mamma Lucia. The villagers pass through the square, singing of spring and love. Santuzza, once Turridu's mistress but later abandoned by him, comes to speak to Mamma Lucia. She asks where Turridu has gone, and Mamma Lucia reluctantly says that he went to get wine in Francofonte. Santuzza replies that this cannot be true, as he was seen in town last night. Alfio, Lola's husband, enters with his cart, singing a merry song (*Il cavallo scalpita* – *The horse paws the ground*), which is echoed by the villagers who have arrived with him. As the people drift away, Alfio asks Mamma Lucia whether she has any more of her good wine. She replies that she has none at the moment, but that Turridu has gone to fetch some. Alfio remarks that this is unlikely: he himself saw Turridu near his house that morning. Mamma Lucia is puzzled and wants to know more, but Santuzza hushes her and Alfio hurries off.

From the church come the hymns of Easter. Santuzza, who has been excommunicated for her affair with Turridu, may not enter, but she joins in singing outside in the square. Mamma Lucia demands to know why Santuzza hushed her when she wanted to ask Alfio about Turridu. In a famous aria (*Voi lo sapete* – *You well know*), Santuzza sings that Turridu has left her to take up an affair with his old love, Lola. Crying that she is damned, she begs Mamma Lucia to go to church to pray for her.

Turridu enters and insensitively asks Santuzza if she is going to church. Their angry dialogue is interrupted by the appearance of Lola herself, who arrives singing a gay melody (*Fior di giaggiolo* – *Fairest of flowers*). She exchanges a few mocking words with Santuzza and Turridu and enters the church. As Santuzza continues to beg Turridu not to desert her, he grows angry and throws her to the ground. Then he rushes off into the church after Lola, as Santuzza screams a curse after him. Still furious when Alfio returns, she warns him of Lola's deceit. He leaves promising vengeance.

An *intermezzo* (an instrumental piece in the middle of an opera) follows, while the stage remains empty, reminding us of the calm of Easter Day. At its conclusion the singing villagers pour out of the church. Lola and Turridu come out together, and Turridu invites the villagers to drink a toast with him (*Viva il vino spumeggiante* – *Here's to the sparkling wine*). As he drinks to Lola, Alfio enters. The women, sensing danger, urge Lola to leave, as Turridu is forced to challenge Alfio to a duel. Alfio leaves to await him at the edge of town. Calling his mother, Turridu tells her that he must leave for awhile; if he does not return she must be a mother to Santuzza. In despair he goes off to meet Alfio. The stage fills with agitated people, and a confused murmuring is heard in the distance. Suddenly a woman screams, '*Hanno ammazzato compare Turridu!*' – '*They've killed Turridu!*'. More people rush in as Santuzza and Mamma Lucia fall down senseless.

Mascagni's reputation is based on this work alone. Of his other six operas only *L'amico Fritz* (*Friend Fritz* -- 1891) is occasionally performed.

Often presented on the same bill as *Cavalleria rusticana* is *Pagliacci* (*The Clowns*), a short *verismo* opera by Ruggiero Leoncavallo (1858–1919). The libretto was written by the composer, who based it on a real-life incident from his boyhood. A group of travelling players arrived in his home town, and after the show an actor murdered his wife. Leoncavallo's father was the judge at the ensuing trial. The play within the play employs the characters of the traditional Italian street theatre (the *commedia dell' arte*): Columbine, Harlequin and the clowns. The opera was first performed at the Teatro dal Verme in Milan on May 21, 1892.

The prelude is introduced by a lively melody depicting a band of strolling players, followed by some of the quieter themes from the opera. A return to the opening theme introduces Tonio, costumed as Taddeo the clown, who walks in front of the curtain to introduce the play to the audience (*Io sono il Prologo* – *I am the Prologue*). He explains that the author of the work about to be performed wished to make use of traditional characters and conventions, but that the substance of the play is the reality of human love and hatred. He leaves calling to the players to begin the show.

Act 1. takes place near a village in Calabria around three o'clock in the afternoon on a church holiday in August. The players have set up a travelling theatre stage, and a huge din arises as the villagers welcome the players. Canio bangs loudly on his drum and invites them all to come to see the play at eleven o'clock that evening. Tonio, the hunchbacked clown, comes to help Canio's wife Nedda down from the players' cart, but the jealous Canio boxes Tonio's ears and helps her down himself. The villagers invite Canio to join them for a drink, and he accepts reluctantly, still suspicious of Tonio, who remains behind. To enact a betrayal on stage is one thing, he says, but if Nedda were to betray him in real life, the story would end quite differently. The villagers leave for

15/10/911

Enrico Caruso (Italian tenor, 1873–1921) as Canio (right) and drawn in a cartoon by himself. Considered one of the most famous tenors of all time, he was the idol of the opera world for more than twenty years. Many recordings were made of his powerful voice which was admired for its expressive shading and enormous range.

Vespers, and Canio goes off with Peppe, another member of the troupe.

Nedda, left alone, is momentarily disturbed by Canio's jealous words, wondering if he is aware that she has a lover. Banishing this unhappy thought, she falls to watching the birds flying in the summer sunshine and envies their freedom (*O che bel sole – O what beautiful sun*). Then the ugly Tonio returns to declare his love for her. When he tries to kiss her, she strikes him across the face with a whip. Screaming that she will pay for her insult, he wanders off.

Silvio, a villager and Nedda's lover, comes to see her. He unsuccessfully tries to convince her that she should remain behind with him when the players move on. Unseen, Tonio returns briefly to observe the pair. Silvio finally overcomes Nedda's objections, and she agrees to meet him that night after the play. Canio and Tonio enter to hear her farewell to him (*A stanotte – e per sempre tua sarò – Until tonight – and I will be yours forever*), but Canio is intercepted by Nedda, and Silvio escapes. Sneering, Tonio promises Nedda that he will be more successful the next time. Canio pulls a dagger on Nedda and demands to know the name of her lover, but she refuses to tell him. Luckily Peppe returns and pulls Canio away from her. Tonio slyly suggests to Canio that he has only to play his part for the evening, as Nedda's lover will certainly return. Tonio and Peppe go to prepare the stage, and Canio is left alone to muse on his unhappiness in one of the most famous tenor solos in all opera (*Vesti la giubba – Put on the costume*): As a clown (*pagliaccio*), his job is to make people laugh while Harlequin and Columbine betray him. He fears that this has become his role in real life as well.

A brief *intermezzo* is performed before Act 2. which takes place in the same location as Act 1. but at night. Peppe blows the trumpet, and Tonio beats the drum. The villagers arrive to take their places for the play. Nedda, dressed as Columbine, is collecting money from the audience. As she passes Silvio she warns him that although he was not identified they must be careful.

The audience quiets down and the play begins. Columbine (Nedda) is seen walking back and forth, annoyed that the servant Taddeo has not yet returned with food. Pagliaccio, her husband, will not be home until late. Harlequin (Peppe) sings a serenade to her outside her window (*O Colombina, il tenero fido Arlecchin – O Columbine, your always faithful Harlequin*). Taddeo finally arrives with the groceries, getting laughs from the audience as he pretends to court Columbine. Harlequin enters and throws him out. As they eat dinner, the two plot their elopement, and Harlequin gives Columbine a sleeping potion to administer to her husband before bedtime. Taddeo comes to warn them that Pagliaccio has unexpectedly arrived home, and Harlequin leaves through the window. Columbine calls after him the same farewell she spoke to Silvio that afternoon (*A stanotte – e per sempre tua sarò*). Canio enters as Pagliaccio, and the play begins to alternate between fiction and the real life drama of Canio's jealousy. The crowd is much impressed by his excellent 'acting'. Finally, taking a knife from the table, he demands the name of Nedda's lover. When she refuses to tell him, he stabs her. Silvio makes his way to the stage as she calls his name for help, and Canio turns to stab him too. As the frightened villagers try to subdue Canio, he drops his knife and sobs, '*La commedia è finita!*' – '*The play is over!*'.

The true successor to Verdi was not, however, either Mascagni or Leoncavallo, but Giacomo Puccini (1858–1924). Born into a musical family in the small Italian town of Lucca, he soon recognized that the only way to wealth and fame for an Italian musician lay in opera composition. At the conservatory in Milan he studied under Amilcare Ponchielli (1834–1886), an opera composer remembered for his *La Gioconda* (1876), and became a friend, and later, a rival, of Mascagni.

His first opera, *Le Villi* (*The Witches* – 1884) won a moderate success, but it was with his third opera, *Manon Lescaut* (1893), that he achieved real fame. This work was based on the novel by Abbé Prévost which had also inspired the French composer Jules Emile Frédéric Massenet (1842–1912) to write an opera, *Manon* (1884), on the same subject.

Puccini's next opera, *La Bohème*, firmly established his position as Verdi's successor. Giuseppe Giacosa and Luigi Illica, who had assisted him with the libretto for *Manon Lescaut*, helped to prepare the libretto for *La Bohème*. The plot is drawn from a novel by Henri Murger (1822–1861), *Scènes de la vie de Bohème* (*Scenes from Bohemian Life* – published 1851), which had also been presented as a play, *La Vie de Bohème* (1849). The first performance of Puccini's opera took place at the Teatro Regio in Turin on February 1, 1896, conducted by the young but soon to be famous Arturo Toscanini. The critics gave the work a lukewarm reception, but the public loved it, and during February alone there were twenty-four sold out performances.

Puccini's style draws elements from the *verismo* approach to opera composition as well as renewing some features of earlier romantic operas. The libretti which he chose tend to be more sentimental than those of Mascagni or Leoncavallo, although there is always an element of suspense in his plots. Exotic settings, whether an artist's garret in Paris or a California saloon, are the rule. The action is less compact than that of the *verismo* operas, but the music maintains a continuous flow with no pauses or low points. Puccini created his own style of musical declamation, in which one note of the melody corresponds to one syllable of the text, with only rare vocal ornaments. The distinction between recitative and aria styles has largely vanished, although there is no question that arias remain as separate numbers within the framework of the scenes.

Melodies tend to follow the scale in their gently flowing movement, and vocal melody is predominant. Puccini was very concerned about variations in *tempo* (speed), and his scores are full of precise information on this point. He had a great interest in the colour effects that can be achieved by the orchestra and used musical themes to unify his operas by creating associations with previous actions. Several other characteristic features are his use of off-beat accompaniments to create a sense of urgency, his use of a long note in the bass (pedal) over which the rest of the musical texture continues, and his use of the old Italian trick of doubling the melody in octaves for emphasis. For special effect he also occasionally doubles the singer's line in the bass of the orchestra.

The action of the opera is set in the Latin Quarter of Paris around 1830. There is no prelude.

Act 1. takes place in a garret room in winter where Marcello, a painter, is working on a large canvas of the Red Sea, while Rodolfo, a poet, is trying to write. It is too cold to work, and Rodolfo suggests that they burn his play for heat. To add to their woes, Colline, a philosopher, enters to tell them that unfortunately all the pawnshops are closed because it is Christmas Eve. As the fire dies, two porters arrive bearing wood, food, wine and cigars. A fourth friend, Schaunard, a musician, enters happily with his gifts. He tries to tell his companions how he got the money, but they are too interested in the food to listen. When he finally gets their attention, he tells them to save this food for later, for tonight they are going out to dinner. Benoit, the old landlord, knocks on the door, demanding the rent. The young men invite him in and offer him wine, playfully accusing him of making love to a pretty girl. When he doesn't deny their sly hints, they charge him with immorality and throw him out, thus avoiding payment. The friends leave for the Café Momus, and Rodolfo promises to join them shortly, after he finishes an article that he is writing. As the sounds of his companions' departure dies away, a timid knock is heard at the door. Mimì enters, hoping to relight her candle, which has been blown out. Breathless from climbing the stairs, she faints. Rodolfo revives her with some wine, and she turns to leave with her lighted candle. As she stands in the doorway the candle goes out again, and Rodolfo deliberately lets his go out as well. Now she cannot find her key, and together the two search the floor, their hands suddenly meeting in the dark. In two long passages of sustained lyricism, Rodolfo and Mimì tell each other about their lives. Rodolfo tenderly exclaims, '*How cold your little hand is!*' (*Che gelida manina*) and introduces himself as a poet who lives in happy poverty. Mimì shyly responds, '*They call me Mimì*' (*Mi chiamano Mimì*), and tells of the artificial flowers that she makes for a living and of her love of springtime and its real flowers.

The famous Italian tenor Luciano Pavarotti sings the role of Rodolfo with Ileana Cotrubas as Mimì in a La Scala performance of *La Bohème*.

Rodolfo's friends call up that they are tired of waiting for him. He tells them to go ahead to the Café, that he will join them shortly. Turning and seeing Mimì in the moonlight, he begins a duet (*O soave fanciulla* – *O sweet girl*) in which he and Mimì sing of their love for each other.

Act 2. takes place at a square in the Latin Quarter surrounded by shops. At one side is the Café Momus. The friends are already there celebrating when Rodolfo and Mimì stroll in. Despite the crowd they have been able to find a table at the Café, and Rodolfo introduces Mimì to them (*Questa è Mimì – This is Mimì*). Rodolfo has bought Mimì a bonnet as a present, which the others admire. A toast is proposed and all drink. Marcello, noticing an attractive young girl in elegant clothes arriving with a pompous old gentleman named Alcindoro, says bitterly that his drink should have been poison. He tells Mimì that the girl's first name is Musetta, but that her last name is temptation. Musetta, noticing Marcello, is annoyed that he won't even look at her. She begins her charming and flirtatious aria (*Quando me'n vo'soletta – When I go by myself*), teasing Marcello for his infatuation with her. When she is sure of his response, she suddenly cries out that her foot hurts and sends Alcindoro out to buy a new shoe. When he is gone, she runs to Marcello. She suggests that as the friends do not have enough money to pay their bill, they should leave it for Alcindoro to pay when he returns. A parade of guards crosses the square, and in the confusion the conspirators run off, leaving the bill for Alcindoro, who returns, picks it up and collapses with shock.

Act 3. takes place near one of the gates of Paris in winter. On one side of the stage is a tavern, whose sign is Marcello's painting of the Red Sea. Musetta's voice comes from within, joining others in a drinking song. Mimì enters, looking for Marcello's place of work, and a helpful guard points out the tavern. When Marcello comes out to see her, she asks him to speak to Rodolfo for her. In a fit of jealousy he has left her, although Mimì knows that he still loves her. When Rodolfo suddenly appears, she hides. Marcello tells him that he is not being fair to Mimì. Rodolfo responds that, although he loves her desperately, he fears that she is dying, and because of his poverty he cannot take care of her properly. Mimì comes to meet Rodolfo, and he urges her to come into the warm inn. She refuses, saying she has only come to say farewell (*Addio senza rancor – Farewell without anger*). A sad duet follows (*Addio, dolce svegliare alla mattina – Farewell, sweet awaking in the morning*), in which they are joined by Marcello and Musetta, who come out of the tavern quarrelling. In the end Rodolfo and Mimì agree to remain together until the spring.

Act 4. takes place in the garret. Marcello and Rodolfo are talking. They have separated from Musetta and Mimì, and both are too depressed to work (*O Mimì, tu più non torni – O Mimì, you won't come back*). Schaunard and Colline enter, bringing a meagre meal of bread and a salted herring. Pretending that they are sitting down to an elaborate feast, the four make merry over their scanty food. They are interrupted by Musetta, who announces that Mimì is coming and that she is very ill. Rodolfo hurries out to help her up the stairs, and the friends assist her to the bed. As Mimì and Rodolfo talk of their reconciliation, Musetta tells the others that Mimì knows she is dying and has come to die with Rodolfo by her side. Marcello agrees to pawn Musetta's earrings to buy medicine and pay a

A scene from *Tosca* with Maria Callas (1923–1977) as the heroine and Tito Gobbi as the treacherous Baron Scarpia. An American soprano of Greek descent, Callas had a spectacular international career. She was admired for her striking beauty and fine acting ability as well as her superb voice.

doctor, and Musetta leaves with him to buy a muff for Mimì's icy hands. Colline takes off his old coat, which is all he has to pawn, and bids it a touching farewell (*Vecchia zimarra, senti – Listen, my old coat*) and convinces Schaunard leave the lovers alone together.

Mimì and Rodolfo now recall scenes of happier days (*Sono andati? – Are they gone?*). Gently Rodolfo takes out the bonnet that he bought for Mimì on Christmas Eve, which he has carried next to his heart since they parted. As they recall how they met, Mimì is seized with a terrible fit of coughing. The others return to report that the doctor will come soon, and Musetta gives Mimì the muff, saying that it is a gift from Rodolfo. Gratefully Mimì sighs that now she will be warm and able to sleep. As Musetta quietly prays for Mimì, Rodolfo steps over to ask if she thinks there is any hope. Schaunard moves to the bed, returning to tell Marcello quietly that Mimì is dead. Colline enters to give Musetta the money from his coat. Rodolfo moves over towards Mimì but is suddenly stopped by the expressions on his friends' faces. He runs to the bed, calling her name again and again.

After *La Bohème*, Puccini's reputation was firmly established, and all of his subsequent works remain in the 20th-century opera repertory. *Tosca* (1900), a suspense-filled melodrama, pits a fiery heroine against the diabolical chief of the Roman secret police, Baron Scarpia, surely opera's most compelling villain. *Madama Butterfly* (1904), in contrast, is the poignant story of a Japanese girl's love for a thoughtless American naval officer. Others are *La fanciulla del West* (*The Girl of the Golden West* – 1910), *La rondine* (*The Swallow* – 1917); and *Trittico* (1918), a trio of short operas: *Il tabarro* (*The Cloak*), *Suor Angelica* (*Sister Angelica*) and *Gianni Schicchi*.

Puccini's last opera was *Turandot*. The musical and dramatic style of this work is stronger and more dissonant than his earlier operas. The chorus has a major role, comparable to that of the chorus of *Boris Godunov*. Turandot herself must have extreme vocal stamina, for her music remains in a high range for long periods of time. To emphasize the exotic setting of the opera, Puccini employed pentatonic (five-note) scales and introduced into the orchestra such instruments as the gong and the xylophone.

The libretto by Giuseppe Adami and Renato Simoni, written in close collaboration with Puccini, is loosely derived from the play *Turandotte* (1762) by the Venetian playwright Carlo Gozzi (1720–1806). Friedrich Schiller (1759–1805) adapted the play and translated it into German. A 20th-century performance with incidental music by Feruccio Busoni (1866–1924) took place in Berlin, and it was this version of the play that was transformed into the libretto of Puccini's *Turandot*.

The opera was not completed by Puccini himself, for he died after completing the scene of Liù's death. Arturo Toscanini, the famous conductor, made arrangements for a friend of Puccini, Franco Alfano (1876–1954), to complete the opera according to sketches made by the composer. The first performance took place at the Teatro alla Scala in Milan on April 25, 1926. There is no prelude to the opera.

Act 1. takes place before the enormous walls of the imperial palace of Peking at sunset. A crowd moves restlessly as a Mandarin reads a proclamation: Princess Turandot will be the bride of the man of royal blood who is able to solve the three riddles which she will pose to him. Should he fail the test, however, he will forfeit his head. The Prince of Persia is to be executed at the rise of the moon. The crowd is delighted by this and begins to surge towards the palace, but they are forced back by the guards. Liù, a young slave girl, kneels beside an old man, Timur, who has fallen in the press of the crowd. A young man, Calaf, goes to her aid and recognizes Timur as his father, the exiled king of the Tartars. The old man gives an account of how Liù rescued him in his flight after the battle. Calaf warns his father not to reveal his identity, since the usurper of the throne still seeks his death. Turning to Liù, he asks her who she is and why she did this good deed. She answers that she is nothing, but that one day in the palace long ago Calaf smiled at her. They help the old man away as the crowd begins a mighty chorus calling for blood. The moon begins to rise and the executioners enter with the Prince of Persia, preceded by a chorus of boys. Seeing that he is such a young man, the mob is moved to pity and calls to the Princess to have mercy on him. Turandot enters on the porch above. All prostrate themselves except the Prince of Persia, the executioner and Calaf, who is struck by her incredible beauty. She does not speak, but merely indicates the death sentence by a gesture. The procession moves on, followed by a group of priests.

Timur, Calaf and Liù are left alone. Still entranced by Turandot's beauty, Calaf tries to strike the gong to announce himself as a suitor, but is held back by Timur and Liù. Next Ping, Pong and Pang, ministers of the Emperor, try to restrain him. Then Turandot's ladies come to the balcony to ask for silence, but in vain. The ghosts of former suitors, who have died in seeking Turandot's hand, appear on the ramparts of the palace demanding that Calaf call her, that they may again hear her voice. Ping, Pong and Pang continue their pleas as the head of the Prince of Persia is carried away by the executioner. Finally Liù begs Calaf to have pity on her and his father (*Signore, ascolta – Listen, Sir*). Unmoved, he tries to reassure her, asking only that she continue to care for Timur (*Non piangere, Liù – Don't cry, Liù*). He strikes the gong three times to announce himself as a candidate. The crowd responds that they are already digging his grave.

Act 2. begins in a Chinese pavilion. Ping, Pong and Pang complain of being overworked by the enormous number of funeral arrangements: they have been reduced to functioning as ministers of the executioner. Unhappily they exit to watch another ceremony which they expect to end in the death of the contestant.

Scene 2. takes place in a square in front of the palace, where a crowd has gathered. Ping, Pong and Pang enter to join the Eight Wise Men and the Mandarins. The Emperor arrives to the cheers of the crowd and vainly tries to dissuade Calaf from risking his life. The Mandarin again reads the fatal decree. Preceded by a chorus of boys, Turandot enters and goes to her throne. She begins an aria (*In questa reggia – In this Palace*) in which she explains that she is taking vengeance against all men for a wicked deed done long ago when a princess was dragged away from this very palace and slain by a foreign prince.

The beautiful Maria Jeritza (Czech soprano, b. 1887) as Princess
Turandot. (New York, 1926)

Then she asks the first riddle: 'What dies each morning and is reborn
each night?' Calaf correctly answers, 'Hope'. She asks the second riddle:
'What is intense as a flame and gives way only with death?' Calaf
correctly answers, 'Blood'. Finally she asks the third riddle: 'Who is
composed of fire and ice, whose freedom is slavery, and whose slavery is
to be a king?' After a terrifying pause, Calaf answers correctly, 'Turandot'. The crowd cheers wildly. Turandot is now frightened in her turn

143

and kneels before her father to beg his protection (*Figlio del cielo* – *Son of Heaven*), but he tells her that the promise is sacred. Calaf, however, offers her an escape: if she can discover his name by dawn, he is prepared to die.

Act 3. begins in the garden of the palace. Heralds announce that by Turandot's orders no one shall sleep in Peking that night. Confident of his secret, Calaf muses that the Princess too shall not sleep (*Nessun dorma!* – *No one sleeps!*). Ping, Pong and Pang enter, moaning that their lives are in his hands. What can they offer him to flee? Everyone will be tortured if they cannot discover his name. Suddenly soldiers drag in Liù and Timur, crying that they have found someone who knows the secret of Calaf's name. All call for Turandot, who appears at once. On her orders, the soldiers begin to torture Timur, but suddenly Liù runs forward, saying that she alone knows the name. Calaf tries to go to her aid but is held back. Even under torture, she refuses to speak. Impressed by her strength, Turandot asks what gives her such courage. She answers that it is love, for which she will sacrifice even her life. Turandot orders the torture to begin again. Unable to escape into the crowd, Liù prophesies to Turandot that she too will learn to love (*Tu che di gel sei cinta* – *You who are girded with ice*). Snatching a dagger from a soldier, she stabs herself and dies. As the crowd bears away her body, Timur slowly follows. Turandot, who is veiled, and Calaf are left facing each other. Calaf commands her to consider the innocent blood that was shed for her (*Principessa di morte!* – *Princess of death!*). Dramatically he tears away her veil and kisses her. Overcome with love, she weeps and admits that she has been defeated (*Del primo pianto* – *My first tears*). In trust he reveals to her his name and places himself in her power. As the trumpets sound, she orders him to come with her before the people.

Scene 2. takes place outside the imperial palace. The Emperor and his court await the results of the trial. Turandot approaches her father's throne and tells him that she now knows the stranger's name. Turning to Calaf, she announces that his name is love. Calaf runs to her and the lovers embrace as the crowd cheers and rejoices.

One of Puccini's contemporaries who produced works of exceptional melodic beauty was Umberto Giordano (1867–1948). His most famous opera is *Andrea Chénier* (1896), which is set against the background of the French Revolution. *Fedora* (1898) is also occasionally produced.

German Opera after Wagner – Strauss

In German opera the tradition established by Weber and brought to a high level of development by Wagner continued unchecked by any reform or counter-movement into the 20th century. Richard Strauss

(1864–1949) was above all responsible for the continuation of this tradition, developing it and adding to it certain dramatic elements characteristic of the Italian *verismo*. His first two operas were strongly reminiscent of Wagner, but his third opera, *Salome*, revealed him to be a composer with a remarkable individual style.

The libretto of *Salome* closely follows the text of the German translation by Hedwig Lachmann of the play *Salome* (1891), by the noted British dramatist Oscar Wilde (1856–1900). The play, in turn, is based on the Biblical account of John the Baptist. Lachmann's translation was in prose, as is the libretto of the opera, an unusual feature to which critics of the time objected. Strauss began work on *Salome* during the summer of 1903, and the première performance took place at the Hofoper in Dresden on December 9, 1905. Although the original play had been condemned by the censors some years before because of its shocking portrayal of decadent sensuality, it was now regularly performed in Germany, and the opera had no difficulty in obtaining a performance permit.

The musical style of this work is elaborate, containing a wealth of harmonic nuance. A variety of orchestral themes and styles reinforce the dramatic content. The vocal lines are written in a form of melodic declamation. Particularly taxing is the title role of Salome. Strauss was especially interested in the capabilities of the female voice, and here he requires almost non-stop singing in a high register. To perform this role successfully, a singer must have considerable dramatic ability as well as a good voice.

The action of the opera takes place in one tense scene on a moonlit terrace outside the banquet hall of Herod, the Tetrarch of Palestine. In the centre of the stage is a huge iron grate which covers the cistern (well) in which the prophet Jokanaan (John the Baptist) has been imprisoned. There is no prelude.

Salome, daughter of Herod's wife Herodias by a previous marriage, is taking part in a noisy feast in the banquet hall. Although he has been warned many times by a young page that she will only cause trouble for him, Narraboth, a young Syrian captain of the guard, cannot refrain from watching her. From the cistern comes the voice of Jokanaan in prophecy (*Nach mir wird Einer kommen, der ist stärker als ich – After me will come one who is greater than I*). No one may see him, for the Tetrarch has forbidden it. Narraboth's attention is distracted as Salome leaves the table and comes out to the terrace, saying that she can no longer bear Herod's lascivious stares. The voice of Jokanaan is heard again, and Salome demands to be told who he is. Realizing that this is the prophet who publicly condemned her mother's morals, she is intrigued and refuses to leave. She continues to ask questions about Jokanaan and

Olive Fremstad, the Metropolitan Opera's first Salome (1907). She
is seen here at the cistern carrying Jokanaan's severed head.

eventually demands to speak with him. At first the soldiers refuse to go
against the order of Herod, but Narraboth is so charmed with her
attentions that he reluctantly brings forth the prisoner. Jokanaan,
brought to the terrace, continues to rail against Herod and Herodias.
Narraboth begs Salome to leave, but she remains, more intrigued than
ever. While Jokanaan exhorts her to go to the desert and repent, she tells
him of her desire for his body, for his hair and finally for his mouth,
which she wishes to kiss. Narraboth, in despair over her words, kills
himself with his dagger and falls between her and Jokanaan. Unmoved
by his death, Salome continues to entreat Jokanaan to permit her to kiss
him. Telling her that she is accursed, the prophet returns to his cistern.

Herod enters, looking for Salome, followed by Herodias and the
court. As he slips in Narraboth's blood and sees the body, he fears that it
may be a bad omen and orders the soldiers to remove the corpse. He
offers Salome wine and fruit, but she is not interested. The voice of
Jokanaan breaks in to announce that the time of which he prophesied is
now come. Herodias complains of the insults that the prophet has offered
her and suggests that Herod turn him over to the Jews who seek his

blood. Herod refuses, saying that Jokanaan is a holy man. The Nazarenes and Jews of the court begin a quarrel about the role of Jesus: Is he or is he not the Messiah? Meanwhile, Jokanaan's voice continues with imprecations against the wanton woman. Herodias, who believes that he speaks of her, begs her husband to have him silenced. Herod ignores her and turns to Salome, asking her to dance for him. She refuses until he offers in exchange to swear an oath to give her whatever she asks of him, up to half his kingdom. The famous 'Dance of the Seven Veils' follows. As it ends, she throws herself at Herod's feet, demanding as her reward the head of Jokanaan on a silver tray. Horrified by the request, Herod tries to bargain with her, but to no avail. As he sinks back in a faint, Herodias, pleased with this turn of events, removes the ring of death from his hand and gives it to a soldier to take to the executioner. Herod, returning to his senses, has a premonition of evil as he misses his ring. Salome waits eagerly by the cistern until the arm of the executioner raises up to her a platter on which lies the severed head of Jokanaan. Salome seizes it with joy, singing that now she will kiss the mouth of the man who rejected her (*Ah! du wolltest mich nicht deinen Mund küssen lassen, Jokanaan! – Ah, you wouldn't let me kiss your mouth, Jokanaan!*). Herod is disgusted by this monstrous behaviour and turns to leave, ordering all the torches to be extinguished. As he ascends the steps to the banquet hall, he turns to look back at Salome, who is singing a mad song of love to the severed head (*Ah! Ich habe deinen Mund geküsst, Jokanaan! – Ah, I have kissed your mouth, Jokanaan!*). Suddenly she is illuminated by a ray of moonlight and in horror Herod orders his soldiers to kill her. They rush forward and crush her beneath their shields.

A similar element of horror appears in Strauss' next opera, *Elektra* (1909), which is based on the Greek myth of a young girl who avenges her father's murder. *Der Rosenkavalier* (*The Cavalier of the Rose* – 1911), written to a charming libretto by Hugo von Hofmannsthal (1874–1929), reflects another side of this gifted composer. This bittersweet comedy is about an older woman who reluctantly yields her young lover to another. In keeping with the character of the libretto is the lighter, more elegant and gilded musical style of this work. Other Strauss operas often performed are *Ariadne auf Naxos* (1912), *Die Frau ohne Schatten* (*The Woman without a Shadow* – 1919) and *Arabella* (1933).

Germany and Austria were blessed with a great wealth of opera composers after the First World War. Among them are Arnold Schönberg (1874–1951), known for originating the twelve-tone method of musical composition (music composed of a repeated series of the 12 notes of the scale), who wrote *Moses und Aron* (premièred posthumously in 1957); Alban Berg (1885–1935), who wrote *Wozzeck* (1925) and *Lulu* (premièred posthumously in 1937); Paul Hindemith (1895–1963), who

wrote *Cardillac* (1926) and *Mathis, der Maler* (Mathis, the Painter – 1938); Carl Orff (b. 1895), who wrote *Antigonae* (1949); and Kurt Weill (1900–1950), who is best known for *Aufstieg und Fall der Stadt Mahagonny* (*The Rise and Fall of the City of Mahagonny* – 1930) and *Die Dreigroschenoper* (*The Threepenny Opera* – 1928), which is derived from *The Beggar's Opera* of 1728.

Twentieth-century Opera in the United States

While the 19th-century opera repertory of the United States was dominated by the works of Europeans, the 20th century has seen operas written by many excellent American composers. Virgil Thomson (b. 1896) is known for *Four Saints in Three Acts* (1933) and *The Mother of Us All* (1947). George Gershwin (1898–1937) wrote a popular opera in the jazz idiom, *Porgy and Bess* (1935). Samuel Barber (b. 1910) has written two notable operas: *Vanessa* (1958) and *Antony and Cleopatra* (1966), which was composed for the opening of the new Metropolitan Opera House at Lincoln Center in New York.

Gian-Carlo Menotti (b. 1911) is the most prolific of contemporary American opera composers. Born in Italy, he emigrated to the United States as a young man. He has worked extensively in opera staging, which may well be the source of the considerable dramatic understanding which characterizes his works. His melodic musical style shows the influence of his Italian forebears, especially Puccini, and although the orchestral accompaniment clearly belongs to the 20th century in harmonic and rhythmic treatment, his music remains dominated by the human voice. A master designer of scenes that build to intense climaxes, he often chooses plots that are humorous and ironic. He prefers to write his own libretti.

Among his many operas, the best known are *Amelia Goes to the Ball* (1937), *The Medium* (1946), *The Consul* (1950), *Amahl and the Night Visitors* (1951) and *The Saint of Bleecker Street* (1954).

Amahl and the Night Visitors is an interesting 20th-century experiment, for it was originally written for television and was premièred by NBC Television Opera Theatre on Christmas Eve, 1951. It can usually be seen on television around Christmas time and is often performed on stage as well. The entire action of the opera takes place in one act, set in a simple

---

Elisabeth Schwarzkopf (German soprano, b. 1915) in Act III of *Der Rosenkavalier* (Covent Garden, 1959). She made her début in 1938 in Berlin and has since become especially well-known for her singing of Mozart and Richard Strauss.

149

Amahl meets the Three Kings. Left to right: King Balthazar
(Michael Langdon), King Melchior (Michael Maurel), King Kaspar
(Edward Byles) and Amahl (Paul Maurel). (BBC Television
production, 1974)

---

shepherd's hut at the time of the birth of Christ. The role of Amahl is
sung by a boy soprano. There is no prelude.

A crippled young shepherd boy, Amahl, sits playing his pipes in front
of his hut, while his mother, a widow, busies herself with domestic tasks
within. She calls to Amahl, but he continues to play his pipes until she
gets quite annoyed and orders him into the house. She asks what kept
him outside, and he answers that he was watching a star with an enormous tail of fire. She thinks this is just another of his incredible stories.
Then, suddenly afraid, she hugs him, wondering if hunger has affected
his mind. She doubts that they will be able to survive unless they turn to

begging. Bidding each other an affectionate goodnight, they lie down to sleep. Out of the distance come the three kings, Melchior, Balthazar and Kaspar. They approach the hut, and Melchior knocks on the door. Amahl is sent to answer it. He quickly returns to his mother, demanding that she come with him so that she may tell him whether what he sees is real. In annoyance she goes to open the door. Seeing the three kings, she bows and welcomes them, but warns that she has very little to offer them. Quickly she goes out to gather wood for the fire, while Amahl remains with the kings to tell them his story. When his mother returns, she sends him to beg food for the kings from the other shepherds. As the kings describe to her the child for whom they are bringing their magnificent gifts, she thinks to herself that the child well might be her own. The other shepherds arrive with food and are thanked for their kindness. As all lie down to sleep, Amahl's mother thinks of the gold brought by Melchior and what it could do for her son, and quietly she creeps over to take it. She is caught by the page, who wakes the kings. Amahl, seeing his mother held by the page, goes at once to her defence. Melchior, touched, tells her that she may keep the gold. The child whom they seek has no real need of it, for He will found His Kingdom on love alone. As the kings prepare to continue their journey, the mother impetuously begs them to take back the gold and laments that she has no gift of her own to send with them. Amahl says that he will send his crutch, which he made himself. As he hands it to the kings, it becomes evident that he no longer has any need of it. Happily he dances around the room as the kings tell his mother that her son is loved by the Son of God. Amahl then begs to go with the kings to see the child, and his mother agrees that he should go to give his thanks in person. Slowly the procession leaves the hut. As Amahl follows them, his crutch tied to his back, he begins to play his pipes.

Opera in Great Britain in the Twentieth Century

Around the turn of the century, Great Britain, like so many other countries, shook itself free from foreign domination in opera, and English composers began to work in this form. Frederick Delius (1862–1934) is best known for *A Village Romeo and Juliet* (1907), and Ralph Vaughan Williams (1872–1958) composed *Riders to the Sea* (1937) and *The Pilgrim's Progress* (1951). The works of both composers were well received in England, but neither was able to establish a significant international reputation.

It fell to Benjamin Britten (1913–1976) to achieve an international success while maintaining a characteristically English style of

composition. The first opera to win this acclaim was *Peter Grimes*, which is written to a text by Montagu Slater after a poem by George Crabbe. The music is contemporary in style, but the structure reveals set numbers connected by sections of recitative similar to the form of pre-Wagnerian 19th-century operas. The scenes and acts are, however, linked by orchestral interludes, meant to be played while the curtain is down. The first performance took place at Sadler's Wells Theatre in London on June 7, 1945. There is no prelude.

The prologue takes place around 1850 in the town hall of Borough, a small fishing village on the coast of East Anglia. An inquest is taking place. Peter Grimes' apprentice has died at sea in suspicious circumstances. The verdict is accidental death, but the assembled townspeople are not convinced of Grimes' innocence. The hall empties and Grimes is left with Ellen Orford, the widowed schoolmistress, who is almost alone in believing Grimes' version of the lad's death. She tries to comfort him, and he finds some reassurance in her company.

A musical interlude ('Dawn') forms the bridge to Act 1. which begins on a street near the sea a few days later. As a group of fishermen arrive and unload their catch, Auntie (owner of 'The Boar') opens her tavern and welcomes the men. Grimes is heard calling for someone to come help him with his boat. The villagers decline to assist him, but Ned Keene, an apothecary with a dubious reputation, and Captain Balstrode, a retired skipper, go to his aid. Keene tells Grimes that he has found him a new apprentice from the workhouse. If Grimes will send over a note, the boy can ride back with Hobson, who is both a carter and the town constable. Hobson, however, will have nothing to do with the project. Only when Ellen arrives and agrees to come with him to pick up the boy does he agree to go. As they leave, Captain Balstrode warns that a storm is coming. The villagers take shelter, concerned that the eroding shoreline will be further eaten away and that some day the entire village will be swallowed up by the sea. Balstrode remains with Grimes and suggests that, given the villagers' suspicions, it would be better for Grimes to go elsewhere and begin his life anew. Grimes, however, says that he intends to remain, to become wealthy and to marry Ellen. As Balstrode leaves him, there is a moment of calm in the storm, and Grimes sings peacefully of Ellen's love for him.

Introduced by a linking interlude ('The Storm'), scene 2. takes place inside the tavern. The storm has caused a landslide behind Grimes'

The vision and the reality: (Above) Composer Benjamin Britten, left, and producer Eric Crozier look at the model set for the village street in *Peter Grimes*; (Below) the same street as a completed set in the opera's first performance. (Sadler's Wells, 1945)

154

cottage, and the road there is underwater. Grimes himself enters, seemingly oblivious of the assembled company, to sing of the stars and fate. Ellen, Hobson and the new apprentice, John, enter soaked to the bone. Grimes leaves at once with the boy.

Act 2. is introduced by an interlude ('Sunday Morning'). The action takes place on the beach, while most of the villagers are in church. Grimes' apprentice, John, plays quietly while Ellen sings of the calm happiness she senses in the day. Suddenly she notices a tear in the boy's coat, and looking more closely, she discovers that he is bruised. Grimes clearly has begun to mistreat the lad. Grimes himself appears to order the boy to go fishing with him, although it is Sunday. When Ellen says that John deserves a rest, he becomes angry and strikes her. As she leaves weeping, he orders the boy to follow him to the boat. Several villagers who have witnessed the scene spread the news, and when Ellen returns she finds that a crowd has gathered. She is asked to explain the situation, but when she tries to defend Grimes, she is shouted down, and a mob of men, led by a drummer, leaves to seek Grimes at his hut. Ellen, Auntie and Auntie's two 'nieces' (bar girls) remain to lament the ways of the menfolk.

Another musical interlude ('Passacaglia') leads into scene 2., which takes place at Grimes' hut. Grimes roughly forces John to prepare for work. Between interludes of reflection on his plans to make a home for Ellen, he pushes the boy to move faster. When he hears the sound of the approaching drum, he panics and pushes the boy and the tackle out of the back door above the cliff. John screams as he falls, and Grimes quickly climbs down after him. The disappointed mob enters to find the hut empty. All leave except Balstrode, who returns to exit by the back door and climbs down the cliff.

Act 3. introduced by another interlude ('Moonlight'), takes place on the beach near the town hall, where a dance is being held. Village people are coming and going. Ellen shows Balstrode John's jersey, which she has found washed up on the beach. A village woman notices that Grimes' boat has returned, and the villagers begin a search for him.

An interlude follows, leading into scene 2., which takes place on the beach in the fog. Now obviously insane, Grimes enters raving. When Ellen and Balstrode arrive, he does not recognize them or even seem to realize that they are there, but instead sings to himself his song about Ellen's love. Balstrode tells Grimes that the only way to escape the vengeance of the village is to take his boat far out to sea and sink it, and he leaves with him to help him launch it.

Peter Grimes (Peter Pears) with his young apprentice in the first production. Pears (English tenor, b. 1910) created the role of Peter Grimes and has long been associated with the music of Britten.

Dawn comes, and the village stirs with the life of a new day. A boat is reported to be sinking too far out to sea for rescue. The villagers appear to be completely indifferent to the event.

This first major success was followed by *The Rape of Lucretia* (1946), *Albert Herring* (1947), *Billy Budd* (1951), *The Turn of the Screw* (1954) and *Midsummer Night's Dream* (1960). All of these works are performed quite frequently, and they have established Britten as one of the leading opera composers of the 20th century.

Fashions in opera come and go, and the favourite composers of one generation are despised by the next. Some attend operas to hear the music, some to enjoy the spectacle and still others to meet their acquaintances. For most opera is an experience to be treasured – the meeting and union of the arts – the union of another world with our own.

Acknowledgments

The author would particularly like to thank Charles Bonheur of the Metropolitan Opera and Helen O'Neill of the Glyndebourne Festival Opera for their invaluable help and advice in connection with the Production section of this book.

The illustrations are reproduced by kind permission of the following: English National Opera page 3; Mansell Collection 7; Keystone Press Agency 10; Metropolitan Opera, New York 11, 15, 16, 17, 19, 25, 105, 114, 127, 146; Guy Gravett (for the Glyndebourne Festival Opera) 13, 22 (top & bottom), 45; Louis Mélançon (for the Metropolitan Opera) 17, 105, 114; J. Heffernan (for the Metropolitan Opera) 25, 127; EMI Electrola GmbH, Köln 26, 27; Donald Southern 31, 36, 61, 65, 94, 113, 140; BBC Hulton Picture Library 32, 39, 63, 78, 89, 96, 110, 118, 124, 134 (top & bottom), 152 (top & bottom), 154; Mary Evans Picture Library 34; Drottningholms Teatermuseum, Stockholm 37; Reg Wilson 38; Houston Rogers 42, 53, 56, 69, 80, 82, 100 (bottom), 120–121, 131, 148; Anthony Crickmay 46; John Garner 50; Raymond Mander & Joe Mitchenson Theatre Collection 59, 74, 129, 143; British Broadcasting Corporation 86, 150; E. Piccagliani, Teatro alla Scala, Milan 91, 138; Archiv für Kunst und Geschichte, Berlin 98, 100 (top), 102; John Vere Brown 107.

We should also like to thank Opera Magazine, London for the loan of the pictures on pages 11, 86, 91, 114, 138 and 140.

Index

159